AF507401

THE
FOUNDER'S
TREADMILL

A FIELD GUIDE TO
OWNING A BUSINESS, NOT A JOB

David Grau Sr., JD

THE FOUNDER'S TREADMILL

A Field Guide to Owning a Business, Not a Job

Contributing Editor: Heather M. Tucker

ISBN: 979-8-9998061-1-6

Business Transitions Publishing, LLC

Lexington, KY (US)

Printed in the United States of America

OTHER BOOKS BY DAVID GRAU SR., JD

The Stewardship Advantage

Building a Profitable and Principled Small Business

(2025)

Acquiring Your Future…

A Primer for Next Generation Professional Service Providers

(2024)

Building With the End in Mind

A Complete Succession Planning Guide for Professional Service Providers

(2023)

Buying, Selling, and Valuing Financial Practices

(2016)

Succession Planning for Financial Advisors:

Building an Enduring Business

(2014)

A Note About
AI (Artificial Intelligence)

This field guide is my sixth work of nonfiction completed over the past twelve years. I do not use artificial intelligence to generate my manuscripts.

This field guide draws on more than thirty years of my personal experience building, operating, advising, and improving founder-dependent small businesses. I also have eleven years of post-high school education including multiple degrees. And while largely informed by my education and experience, this field guide also reflects the significant contributions of many others I've worked with over that time, and learned from, and to whom I am most grateful.

AI was utilized in refining this manuscript, serving as an editorial tool for research, organization, and draft review. In addition, careful human editing, along with the thoughtful feedback from a team of resilient early readers further strengthened the final work. This is the process, I think, of writing a book in the 21st century.

Table of Contents

INTRODUCTION

UNDERSTANDING THE PROBLEM

CHAPTER ONE	Those First Steps On The Treadmill
CHAPTER TWO	My *Two* Treadmills (A Founder's Story)
CHAPTER THREE	How You Became The System
CHAPTER FOUR	Choosing Your Path
CHAPTER FIVE	Why We Stay On The Treadmill

A FIVE-YEAR PLAN FOR BUILDING A DURABLE BUSINESS

YEAR ONE	BUILD THE FOUNDATION
UPGRADE NO. 1	Get Specific About What You Want
UPGRADE NO. 2	Set Up The Proper Entity And Tax Structure
UPGRADE NO. 3	Install A Professional Cash-Flow System
	Year One Checklist Build The Foundation (Year One: Upgrades 1 Through 3)

YEAR TWO	CREATE STABILITY
UPGRADE NO. 4	Get The Business Out of Your Head
UPGRADE NO. 5	Make Your First Leverage Hire
UPGRADE NO. 6	Install Simple Controls And Accountability
	Year Two Checklist Create Stability (Year Two: Upgrades 4 Through 6)

YEAR THREE	BUILD THE OPERATING SYSTEM
UPGRADE NO. 7	Write Your Mission Statement
UPGRADE NO. 8	Build A Monthly Scoreboard
UPGRADE NO. 9	Professionalize Your Client Service Model
	Year Three Checklist Build The Operating System (Year Three: Upgrades 7 Through 9)

YEAR FOUR   **BUILD CAPACITY & AUTHORITY**

    UPGRADE NO. 10   Build The Growth Engine

    UPGRADE NO. 11   Scale With Systems

    UPGRADE NO. 12   Make Your First Capacity Hire

                             Year Four Checklist Build Capacity & Authority (Year Four: Upgrades 10 Through 12)

YEAR FIVE   **BUILD INDEPENDENCE & OPTIONS**

    UPGRADE NO. 13   Transfer Authority, Not Just Tasks

    UPGRADE NO. 14   Think Like An Owner-Investor

    UPGRADE NO. 15   Address Continuity And Succession Planning

                             Year Five Checklist Build Independence & Options (Year Five: Upgrades 13 Through 15)

LOOKING BACK

LEARNING TO BE AN OWNER (AND CEO)

    CHAPTER SIX   Stepping Off The Treadmill

    CHAPTER SEVEN   Remote vs. Absentee Ownership

    CHAPTER EIGHT   Leadership (In A Nutshell)

    CHAPTER NINE   How Does Your Story End?

A CLOSING THOUGHT

ABOUT THE AUTHOR

APPENDIX

To my grandson, Anthony

There will be times when life feels like you're running on a treadmill.
Lots of effort, not so much forward progress.
Keep going, but make a plan to keep improving yourself.
The man you are becoming matters more than the speed at which you arrive.
I believe in you.
Always.

INTRODUCTION

The founder's treadmill doesn't start out as a problem.

It starts as a victory. You begin with nothing but courage. You build. Clients or customers arrive. Money starts to flow. And for a fleeting moment, you think, "I've got this!" But a month later, it's still you against the world. So you do what all founders do: YOU RUN!

You run as if everything depends on you – because it does. Every step, every choice, every risk writes the story of what it truly means to be a founding owner of a small business. The days are full, and long. If faith in the future could be seen, it would look like one person turning on the lights before dawn and betting on themselves again.

And without even noticing it, the treadmill becomes your operating system. You depend on it every day. It is personal! You are the workflow, the decision-maker, the quality-control gatekeeper. Everything depends on you, the business grows and eventually, inevitably, you hit the stall point. The time will come when you cannot work any harder, or find any more hours in the day, no matter how hard you try. Yet, as your business grows, it demands more of you, so you run a little faster, you try to push through – on a grade that only grows steeper.

If those sentences sound too familiar, you're in the right place. What you need next isn't more effort; it's a smarter design, with a practical way to implement it (while you keep the lights on and your income stream flowing).

I've written this as a field guide, not a book. It's intended to be practical, tactical, and operational, and a quick resource over the years. It's designed to help overwhelmed owners make progress in the middle of real life and hard work, not merely absorb ideas they hope to apply someday. I hope that you will use the pages that follow to:

- Identify where you are (what's working and what's not),

- Decide where you want to go, and

- Take action that moves you forward at a sustainable pace and with minimal disruption.

In terms of efficiently leading you through these steps and your many options, here is how this field guide is laid out:

- **Chapters 1 through 5: Understanding the Problem** — is designed to help you see the treadmill clearly in terms of its strengths, its hidden costs, and the alternatives in front of you.

- **A Five-Year Plan** — gives you the mechanics of the process: fifteen Upgrades over five years, sequenced so that you can implement them while still running your business and making a living. Alternatively, you can implement only those Upgrades that suit your needs while staying on that treadmill and running smarter, with a good plan.

- **Chapters 6 through 9: Learning to be an Owner (and CEO)** — is about owning what you've built, protecting it, transitioning it, and providing the necessary leadership to make sure the last chapter of your career is the one you planned for, not the one that happens to you.

My goal is to give every reader at least a basic diagnosis, a mirror to look into, a language to explain the challenges, and a clear path forward that can adapt to your needs. For what it's worth, I think legacy and meaning are just as important as getting bigger.

Along the way, I'm going to share my story because I started where many founders do. For too long, as I'll explain in Chapter 2, I happily ran on my treadmill in both of my small businesses, unaware that practical and better options existed. I'll uncover the blind spots, point out the wrong turns, and explore the changes that made a real and lasting difference, and helped me retire with both pride in what I built and real financial freedom. (If you'd rather start with the narrative, feel free to read Chapter 2 next and circle back to Chapter 1 to better understand the problem.)

My hope is that as you continue to read, you'll recognize yourself in these pages and feel less alone, and perhaps a little less stuck. There is no perfect small business and no perfect owner. We all do our best. But that doesn't mean you can't build something better. In fact, it may be far better than you think.

Let's get to work.

$$\star\ \star\ \star\ \star\ \star$$

UNDERSTANDING THE PROBLEM

Those First Steps On The Treadmill

If you wake up one morning and realize you're running on the founder's treadmill, it's a sign you've been building with everything you've got. You started the way most small business owners start: by relying on your intelligence, grit, and sheer effort to make it work. Income starts to flow, and your hard work is rewarded. Often, there is just no better way.

Certainly, that's not failure — it's how most small businesses begin. The founder's treadmill is a business model where growth depends on the founder doing, basically, everything. But eventually, **many founders have a difficult time keeping up with the demands of growth and success**. And understanding how a different system could make a real difference is difficult to see when you're already too busy.

The point of this field guide is to help you do three things with clarity and efficiency:

1) See your current situation for what it is,

2) Decide what you actually want your business to do for you, and

3) Make any needed structural improvements that move you toward that goal without impeding your income stream. Those improvements could be minimal or significant.

CHAPTER ONE: THOSE FIRST STEPS ON THE TREADMILL

Having control and making smart choices is what most founders want. That's why the treadmill is such a strange experience when you stop to examine it. If the founder's treadmill has a sound, it is the silence of carrying too much for too long. If you're on that treadmill, you'll likely recognize some of these signs:

- The business relies too heavily on you for decisions, relationships, quality control, and/or sales.

- You can't take time off without feeling anxious, or without something falling apart.

- You're the bottleneck, you know it, but you don't know how to fix it without risking harm.

- Revenue is rising, but your stability and comfort aren't.

- You've done well, but it is hard to grow any larger because you have nothing left to give.

- Your team needs you constantly because the system doesn't hold together without you.

- You want your team to come to you for input and approval on every important decision.

- You're busy all day, but the most important work, such as long-term thinking, planning, marketing, building scale, etc., never gets done.

The *treadmill business model* builds strength, instincts, and survival capacity. It takes courage to start running, to launch a business, and to figure it out as you go. It also takes courage later to make an adjustment and shift to a strategy that can carry you growing small business into the future. Both paths are part of the founder's journey, and I write this with genuine respect for what you've done, and for the fact that you're reading this now. And, of course, there are more choices than just *either/or*.

This field guide is not about your work ethic. In fact, ironically, the stronger your work ethic, the more likely you are to experience the perils of the founder's treadmill. The treadmill is the **Setup-Grow-Struggle-Stall** cycle many founders live inside of for years, sometimes for an entire career, without having the language or perspective to describe it or diagnose it.

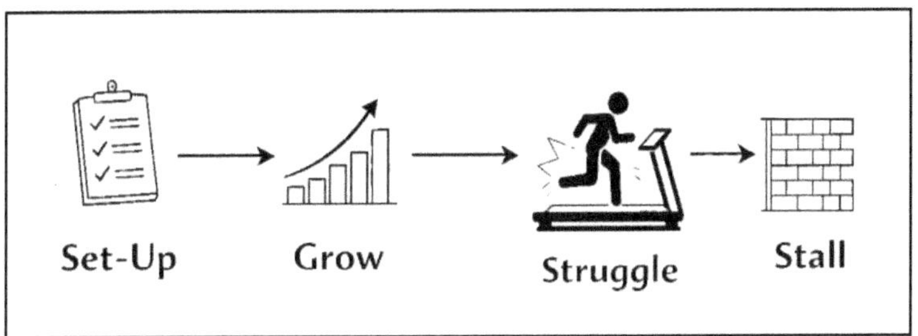

When a business struggles or stalls, it feels like a personal failure, so we don't talk about it much or ask questions soon enough. But it isn't a moral or intellectual weakness. It's a structural trap. Running hard generates income, but it doesn't usually generate durability, so entrepreneurs do what entrepreneurs do: they run even harder in search of a solution.

Let's continue to put this into perspective. Starting a small business is incredibly hard, and while it can be deeply rewarding, it is not for the faint of heart. Historical data from the U.S. Bureau of Labor Statistics (BLS) offers some sobering benchmarks:

- About 20 percent of new businesses do not survive their first two years.

- Roughly 45 percent close their doors and fail within five years, and

- Approximately 65 percent do not make it to year ten.

In other words, nearly two-thirds of small businesses are gone within a decade; there will be nothing to retire from. That is not meant to discourage you. It is meant to prepare you. Courage and determination matter, but are rarely enough on their own. That is why this field guide exists.

Of course, businesses fail for many reasons, usually through a cascade of events rather than one cataclysmic mistake or misjudgment. Aside from a lack of capital or cash flow, **one of the most common forms of fragility is founder-dependency.** And that is why the treadmill is so hard to diagnose and put into context. It saves you for a while, when it feels like nothing else possibly could, and then the hard work that got you *here* seems to work against you in getting *there*.

To be fair, I will zealously argue that founder-dependence is also one of the biggest reasons many small businesses succeed early. On the positive side of the BLS statistics, about 80% of new businesses make it past year two! And I'd guess that many of these entrepreneurs are first-time owners. The founder's treadmill compensates for missing systems, missing people, and missing capital. In the face of every obstacle, including inexperience, stands a resolute owner who will get up early and just figure it out.

The issue is that the very thing that gets you through the early years will quietly become the ceiling you can't break through. **Founder-dependence doesn't announce itself as a problem.** It disguises itself as commitment, competence, and caring. It feels responsible. It feels like leadership. And for a long time, it works well. Until it doesn't.

That same founder-dependency becomes one of the biggest contributors to fragility over time. It drives burnout, delays systems, blocks delegation, slows decisions, and prevents a business from building real capacity. It makes a stall, or a permanent plateau, feel inevitable. The harder you work, individually, the sooner and more surely that day will come.

In 30+ years of building and consulting on small businesses, I have observed first-hand that the size of a small business does not determine how or why you may be running full speed on the founder's treadmill. I have had clients organized as S-corporations with a single owner and 15 hardworking, dedicated employees, yet almost every decision required founder approval or involvement. In contrast, I've seen businesses with one founder and two or three staff members well on their way to creating the systems and processes to be founder-independent within a few years.

If durability and longevity are your goals and you want to build something that can last the length of your career, and beyond, you eventually have to step off (or mostly off) the treadmill and build a business that can carry its own weight, financially and structurally. It needs to grow beyond what any one person can do. It needs to be investable and founder-dependent models rarely fit that bill. You also need a business that can attract, reward, and retain talent. This field guide is written to help you do all this and more.

Three legitimate paths forward. The strategies in this field guide are not as simple as *on the treadmill* or *off the treadmill*. Business doesn't work that way, even though small business founders do tend to think in aggressive, get-things-done terms: either I keep carrying everything, or I make a dramatic move. I can sell, shut down, step away, "fire myself," add a partner, maybe find an investor. Consider that there is often a better way to regain control of your workday and your career, and that is **structural change.** This is not about blowing up what you've built, but redesigning it so your business can start to work for you, rather than you working for it. If success had a stronger form, it would look like a business that can finally work for its owner.

In this field guide, I'll help you explore three legitimate paths (note that you will see a more detailed version of these three paths in Chapter 4: *Choosing Your Path,* along with more context.) These paths are an integral part of this field guide, so remember them or dog-ear this page – not sure how you do that digitally!

1) **Stay founder-dependent intentionally** because it fits your goals and your season of life.

2) **Run it smarter (the middle ground)** by implementing a handful of the most impactful Upgrades that will reduce founder dependency and eliminate the worst of the friction while you keep running and earning a good living.

3) **Step off the treadmill entirely and build a founder-independent business** with real, transferable and realizable value.

All three paths are perfectly valid. The fifteen Upgrades in the second part of this field guide are a toolkit, not a mandate and not a judgment. Use what fits your situation to get where you want to go. I promise to help you with that in the pages that follow.

Entrepreneurs are perfectly wired for any of these choices if the problem is clear, the timing makes sense, and the pathway forward is practical. The challenge is that most founders know only one way to operate, and they're too busy to see, let alone explore any other avenue.

I know because I was one of them.

* * * * *

CHAPTER TWO

My *Two* Treadmills
(A Founder's Story)

In 1994, I opened my first small business as a sole proprietorship. This was a dream I'd carried with me since I was a teenager and watched my father work on his small businesses. At the time, I was a young securities lawyer, newly admitted to the bar, after spending several years as a State of Oregon Securities Regulator while putting myself through law school. I was married with two young children, a mortgage, and my student loans were coming due. It was time to earn a living on my own terms, and I was well-motivated.

I launched with a simple, cost-efficient marketing plan. I wrote, printed (on a dot-matrix printer using WordPerfect® in those days), and mailed a hand-signed letter, with a professionally designed business card enclosed, to every financial professional I used to regulate in the Pacific Northwest. I sent 100 letters a day for a month at $0.29 postage each. Two days after I dropped the first letters in the mailbox, the calls started coming in, and I felt equal parts relief and panic. It was working, I had clients and things to do… now what?!

And that is when I stepped onto the founder's treadmill for the first time. It was a dream come true.

From that day on, I worked ten to twelve-hour days and did everything myself. At the end of the day, I'd go home and work a few more hours after dinner. If determination were a living thing, it would look like one person building a business from nothing. For the first year or two, it honestly felt great. I was learning fast, making a living, and building something that was mine. After eleven straight years of working full- time and going to school full-time, long hours weren't a sacrifice; they were my default setting. My work ethic, I determined, was going to be my secret weapon.

Eventually, I started building a small team to support my growing practice. My first leverage hire (lots more information on that term to come) was a wonderful lady named Jeanie. She was a single mom with enough energy to light up a small city and the kind of work ethic you can't teach. And she could type like the wind (yes, we used electric typewriters in those days). We clicked, the practice grew, and the years moved fast. Being a lawyer is actually really hard work. People hear $300/hour and think lawyers are all overpaid and rich, but I never got to the point where I could, in good conscience, bill more than 3 or 4 hours a day. Still, I gave it everything I had.

What I didn't understand then is what many founders don't understand until it hurts. The treadmill isn't just a business issue. It's a human one. It strains marriages, health, friendships, and the lives of the people who depend on you and your decisions. You run faster as the incline gets steeper… until your energy starts to wane, and then, instinctively, you dig even deeper. Hard work solves everything until it doesn't.

And when a small business fails or its founder burns out and closes the doors, the world quickly summarizes it as a personal failure. "They didn't make it." "They couldn't hack it." But most owners aren't playing with house money. They may begin with a what-have-I-got-to-lose mentality, yet the truth is they have everything on the line. And that is a lot of pressure on top of the workload for as long as it lasts.

About five years into my securities law practice, a client invited me into a second venture as an equity partner in exchange for my legal and securities expertise. The idea was early-internet ambitious: an RMLS® (Residential Multiple Listing System)-style platform for independent financial service professionals. The goal, more or less, was to build "E-Harmony® for financial advisors." This was to be an internet-based business that would basically run itself (yes, people really believed that back in the early internet years!). I became one of five equal owners, and I woke up excited every single day, even as I continued to build my law practice. Life was very, very full back then. What could possibly go wrong?

In hindsight, here's one lesson I learned the expensive way. Never go into business with four strangers as equal partners, even if it's free and there is nothing but upside. It rarely works, and this was no exception. Within a year, internal friction and too much uncompensated work had several partners looking for an early exit. As for me, I saw something much bigger and better on the horizon than my small, time-consuming law practice. So, two of us partners bought out the other three, and a couple of years later I bought out my one remaining partner and took full control. I could see what was *over the horizon*, and I was convinced I could make it work in a big way. I did not suffer from lack of confidence!

The problem was what it required of me.

For a while, I juggled my law practice and the unending demands of this new nationwide business, working more hours than I care to admit. The treadmills (note the shift to plural) moved faster and got a lot steeper. I kept pace, but just barely, working seven days a week. It wasn't noble; it was simply the only way I knew. One business paid the bills, and the other was my hope for an early retirement. And because I had signed off on a significant buyout of that last partner, motivation was once again not an issue. My wife thought I was crazy. She never said those words, but I knew that look.

I remember that first Monday after the buyout papers were signed off on and that last partner was gone. I remember it as if it were yesterday. I was elated by my vision of the future, and by the feeling of total control-work hours notwithstanding. Instead of four partners to contend with, everything routed through me. I was king of the world, or at least my small corner of it. I turned my second treadmill up to a faster, steeper setting and ran full speed quite happily!

Jeanie was still my number one and only employee, and together we kept everything moving... somehow. It was fun and rewarding, and exhausting all at once. I made a good living. And because everything ran through me, I felt needed, important, in total control, and successful – which is exactly why the treadmill is so hard to see for what it is. **It's a great way to start a small business and survive, but it very quickly and quietly becomes a job with overhead.**

Eventually there was no room left in my life for the law practice, and it could never keep pace financially with the new venture. So, I sold my law practice and reinvested the proceeds into the new business, which, not surprisingly, had an unending appetite for cash and time.

Looking back on the treadmill aspect, the core issue had been there all along. I had a time-and-energy problem in my first business, the law practice, and I never actually solved it. I just outworked it and never quite hit the proverbial ceiling. I told myself that as my skills improved and my billing rates increased over the years, I'd gain better control of the situation. But as I learned, a founder-centered business doesn't gradually "free you up" on its own. That never happens. It just quietly moves faster and faster and consumes whatever you're willing to give it.

And because my law practice was never going to be worth much beyond the income it produced, I didn't think in terms of building transferable value. Instead, I thought in terms of keeping the machine fed. This just reinforced the "run faster" mentality. And I had a mortgage to pay. The treadmill served my purposes well, and I liked being in total control. I really liked that part!

In my second small business, I repeated the founder-centered model out of habit without a second thought, only with loftier ambitions. This time I wanted to build something with real value, the eight figures kind of realizable business value, that I could one day sell and step away from. I had that goal from day one. I just didn't know how to get there, so I fell back on what came naturally: work harder, control everything, push through, and grow, grow, grow. Plus, as I paid out debt service on the last partner buy-out, I needed to save money. I had no complaints at the time.

And for a good while, it all worked. Perhaps a better way to say that is, "I made it work," so well that it disguised the problem for me once again. I never saw the issues that were developing, or at least none that I couldn't solve. Eventually, however, I ran headlong into a problem that I would have seen coming if I had taken time to think and plan. **I simply wanted a lot more than a founder-dependent system could ever deliver.** That's obvious to me now. It wasn't obvious then. So let me walk you through the mechanics of it.

In our first year of the "E-Harmony® business model," we grossed around $100,000. We doubled that in year two, doubled again by year four, and again by year six. From the outside, it must have looked like a rocket ship. From the inside, I saw no end in sight, though the business was becoming increasingly fragile because I, alone, was the entire throughput system. Everything routed through me, even as I added help. I had to be in that office every day, or at least on the phone with my team members constantly if on the road. I didn't take a vacation for seven years during this period.

When the business eclipsed $1 million in annual gross revenue, I felt like I could do anything. In truth, I was at that stall point in the aforementioned cycle. Every meaningful decision required my involvement. I worked constantly, just to keep up. I knew I needed to build something scalable, but I didn't know where to start, and I had no time to think or to work on such matters. It never occurred to me that I was the limiting factor – I was the person who made everything go! But we could go no further. I was exhausted.

So I brought in an outside consultant for help, someone smarter and more experienced than me in these matters; I was in my mid 40's at this time. He studied our business carefully and took A LOT of notes. He spent a couple of months interviewing staff, listening in on calls, watching me close deals and solve every problem that arose. Finally, this consultant walked into my office, closed the door rather firmly and said, "Stop it. Just stop it. This is never going to work. Everything can't depend on you."

I bit my tongue. I was shocked, and maybe a little offended. No one had ever said that to me before. I was quite used to being the smartest person in the room. In my mind, it all worked *because of me*. But after thinking about it, and after many conversations with him over the months to come, I had to admit he was right. And that was the beginning of many important changes to come. In fact, over the following years, it changed everything.

The point is, you can't fix what you can't see, and most new or newer small business owners are too busy to focus on their business structure. Once I finally understood what was happening, **I put my ego aside, and we designed a plan to get me off the founder's treadmill**, completely and as quickly as possible. Executing the mechanics I've laid out in the Five-Year Plan, which was my path forward, wasn't the hardest part. The hardest part was changing who I was in the business, what I did, what I controlled, and what I had to let go of. As I look back, those changes should have started in year one or two, not year six or seven. I just didn't know what I didn't know, and, honestly, I enjoyed being the center of my small business.

I'm telling you my story for one reason: **so you can see the treadmill sooner than I did.** Most founders don't recognize it until they start to struggle and then hit the stall point, that moment when effort stops working and "just push harder" becomes the problem instead of the solution. If you want everything you can get out of your small business, and nothing changes, you will eventually reach that point. The takeaway is don't wait to start – make the important changes sooner and save yourself a lot of unnecessary time, money, and energy.

Just know that you're not alone. You have options. Some owners will want to step off the treadmill completely. Some will prefer to redesign it and run it smarter, and a little more efficiently. Either way, the first job is the same: see the structure clearly, decide what you want, and build a system that can support it while still earning a living from the business you've started.

And that brings us to the next step. Before you can change the treadmill business model, or leave it behind, it helps to better understand how and why it gets built: how a founder quietly becomes the workflow, the decision-maker, the quality-control gatekeeper, and the relationship hub… and then never changes. There is a reason for that.

That's what the next chapter is about: **how you became the system.** And it's usually no accident.

* * * * *

CHAPTER THREE

How You Became The System

Most founder-dependent businesses run on the same operating system, even if the industry, service, or profession is completely different. That operating system is not written down. It is not in a policy manual. It does not appear in QuickBooks or on a balance sheet.

It lives in one person. And if you are reading this field guide, it is probably living in you.

That does not make you unusual, and it does not make you a bad owner. In the beginning, founder-centeredness is often necessary. The business starts with one short decision chain, one set of instincts, and one overriding goal: make it work. But over time, what begins as necessity quietly becomes structure. That is how you become the system.

As you've now read, in a founder-dependent business, the founder becomes the workflow, the decision-maker, the relationship hub, the quality-control gatekeeper, and the person every meaningful question eventually reaches. The business runs through a person rather than through a designed structure.

The simplest way to picture it is as a hub-and-spoke wheel, like the one on a bicycle. Everything routes through the center, and the center is you. Employees, contractors, customers, problems, and opportunities all circle around the hub. You can hire two people or twenty, and the routing system often remains unchanged. That is by design, whether intentionally or by default.

Once you see the wheel, however, you'll likely start to notice its symptoms everywhere. Decisions come back to you. Exceptions wait for you. Clients want you. Staff members check with you. Problems pause until you weigh in. Even growth often increases the pressure because more activity still flows through the same center hub.

This is one reason founder-dependence can feel so rewarding and so exhausting at the same time. For many small business founders, it is aptly named **the Identity Trap**.

For many founders, the issue is not only structural. It is personal. Founders do not just run the business, they often get a big part of their identity from being needed, from being the fixer, from being the one who makes everything go. That is one reason founder-dependence can be hard to unwind even after it becomes obvious. Feeling indispensable can feel meaningful. It can feel earned. It can even feel safe – in addition to surviving!

But when your identity is tied to being indispensable, you may build a business that cannot grow without your constant sacrifice. That is fine if it is a deliberate choice. It is a problem if it is simply the default setting. This isn't the end of the story, of course, as to how you became *the system.* It is just the beginning, because as a business grows and demands increase, most founders make the most logical next move:

They hire help. It's the obvious solution.

And this brings us to **the Capacity Illusion.** Hiring help is often necessary in a growing small business; it can bring immediate relief. But hiring help does not automatically create capacity. More often than not, it creates the illusion of capacity.

This is where many founders get fooled. They start to feel overwhelmed, so they add employees or contractors and assume they are building independence, or building smartly in the right direction. Sometimes they are, but more often, they're adding activity that still depends on them, as the founder, to direct, approve, solve, and decide.

That was true in my own businesses. I hired much-needed help and thought I was building scale. What I did not understand at first was that all of that help was still organized around me, and through me as the hub of the wheel. Whether intentionally or inadvertently, we often design our small businesses this way. My entire staff was supporting a founder-centered design, not replacing it. That is the capacity illusion. Here is the distinction that matters:

Help looks like:

- an assistant to you

- a part-time person

- another set of hands

- someone to take a few things off your plate

Capacity looks like:

- clear roles

- decision rights

- standards and checklists

- training to solve problems

- systems and predictable processes

- people who can operate without waiting for the founder's daily approval

If you hire help but keep all the decisions, you bought relief, not durability. In fact, you may actually increase complexity and inefficiency because more people now need direction from you. That is why many fast growing businesses still feel strangely fragile. The founder has more people around them, but the business is still routing through the same central point. The design has not been adapted to the business's needs and trajectory.

Two common patterns show up again and again. The first is the **assistant trap**: you hire someone to make your day easier, but that person becomes a traffic controller for decisions you still make. The second is the **delegation boomerang**: you delegate the task, but the judgment, approval, and accountability keep coming back to you. Neither pattern creates real capacity.

The takeaway is this: help becomes capacity when authority moves. The uncomfortable truth is this: real capacity means someone besides the founder must be empowered to make decisions and influence results. Not occasionally. Every day.

Of course, that raises a valid fear. What about mistakes? What about wasted time, wasted money, or damage to the brand? Those concerns are real, and I've experienced all of them! So, do not jump from "I decide everything" to "Do whatever you think is best." Instead, use some form of an authority ladder such as this:

1) **Do and report:** "Handle it and tell me what you did."

2) **Recommend:** "Bring me your recommendation and the reasons why."

3) **Decide within limits:** "You can decide up to $XX, or within these boundaries."

4) **Own the outcome:** "This result is yours. I'll review it at set intervals."

This is how help becomes capacity without gambling your business, reputation, and income. People need boundaries, standards, and feedback, but they also need room to grow. Real empowerment is not abandoning oversight. It is moving decisions outward in a controlled and deliberate way.

A durable business is not a wheel with the founder at the hub. It is a network of accountable roles connected by systems. Authority is distributed. Processes are documented. Knowledge is transferred. The founder is still important, but no longer central to every transaction.

Finally, the question is not whether you should hire. The question is whether you are willing to let the business eventually operate without you at the center of every important decision, key relationship, and recurring problem. That answer does not depend on headcount. It depends on design.

And that leads directly to the next question: How much of this, and what parts, do you actually want to change?

* * * * *

CHAPTER FOUR

Choosing Your Path

Not every founder wants the same outcome. Not every business should be built the same way. And not every owner needs or wants a business that can run with little or no dependence on them.

That is important to say clearly and respectfully.

Some founders want complete control, some flexibility, a good income, and the satisfaction of doing meaningful work their own way for as long as they choose to do it. Others want to build a strong team, reduce the daily pressure, and buy back meaningful time without trying to build a large enterprise. Still others want durability, independence, transferable value, and perhaps one day a business that can continue without them or be sold or transferred for maximum value.

These are not the same goals. And because they are not the same goals, they do not require the same design or operational structure. One of the most common mistakes a founder can make is assuming that there is a "right way" to build a small business. There is not. Some owners should remain highly involved and founder-centered by design. Some should build a middle path that reduces pressure and increases resilience without fully stepping away, or giving up control. And some should deliberately and immediately build toward a business that can function, grow, and eventually transition beyond the founder. All three paths, and many variations, are fully legitimate.

What is not legitimate is drifting into a model you never consciously chose. That happens all the time. A founder starts with one set of hopes, one set of assumptions, and one level of energy. Then the years pass and the business grows. People are hired. Revenue increases. Complexity rises. Responsibilities accumulate. And without ever meaning to, the founder ends up in a model that does not match their goals, their stage of life, or the future they thought they were building. That is not a strategy. That is drift.

This chapter is about purposefully replacing drift with a measured choice.

Before we talk about systems, structure, or the Five-Year Plan, you need to know what you are aiming at. Otherwise, every improvement will feel random. You may spend time and money solving the wrong problem, or building toward an outcome you don't even want. It is your business, after all, and it needs to work for you. So let me offer three broad paths for you to consider.

> PATH ONE: STAY FOUNDER-DEPENDENT ON PURPOSE.

Some businesses are built around the founder and will remain that way by choice. The owner wants control. The owner likes being central to the work. The business may provide an excellent living, have a strong reputation, and provide years of satisfaction. It may never become highly transferable, but that may not matter much if the founder's goal is income, autonomy, and personal involvement rather than independence or salability.

If this is your preferred path, choose it with knowledge of the benefits and limitations. Your income may depend heavily on your continued effort, without which your income may cease. Your time away from the business may remain limited. The business may be difficult to transfer. Its value may well be tied more to your labor than to the strength of any operating system.

This path works best when the founder is honest about those tradeoffs and builds the business accordingly. That may mean keeping the operation simpler, limiting complexity, protecting margins, and resisting growth that adds pressure without adding enough benefit. It is a valid model, but it works best when it is chosen on purpose rather than drifted into, or started and run, by default.

And all that said, I will be the first to admit that this is a total success. This is not a failure. It is simply a different model, and it should be understood as such. Some days, as I look back on my own career, I really miss this pathway.

>> PATH TWO: RUN IT SMARTER.

This is the path I suspect most founders really want, even if they have never said it aloud. Small business owners do not necessarily want to build a large enterprise or step back from the business they started. But they do want less chaos, less bottleneck pressure, more capable help, better visibility, more control over cash flow, and a business that does not fall apart the moment they step away for a few days or even a few weeks.

This path is about reducing founder-dependence without pretending the founder no longer matters. It is about buying back time, lowering risk, increasing consistency, and creating a stronger operation – and those are some incredibly important goals for a small business to attain. The founder is still very much involved, but not in quite the same exhausting way. **For many readers of this field guide, this is probably the most realistic and attractive path to implement.**

This middle path is not a half-measure. It is a deliberate decision to strengthen the business without pursuing full founder-independence. In practice, that usually means fixing the foundations first: the right entity and tax structure, a clearer cash-flow system, documented core processes, and at least one leverage hire that begins buying back meaningful founder time. Those changes alone can make a business materially stronger, less fragile, and easier to own, even if the founder remains central to some of the work. A specific list of the recommended Upgrades for this path is provided in Year One of the Five-Year Plan.

This path is not about stepping away. It is about stepping back just enough to breathe, think, and lead better. It often produces a business that is more orderly, more resilient, and more enjoyable to own, without requiring a total reinvention of everything you have built. I wish I had known that this was a possibility when deciding to step off my own treadmill.

>>> PATH THREE: STEP OFF THE TREADMILL COMPLETELY.

This path is the most ambitious. It aims at building a business that can function well, create durable value, and potentially outlast the founder. That may mean preparing for eventual sale, succession, shared equity ownership, or a business that can keep growing without the founder carrying the daily operational load.

This path requires the most structural work. It requires better systems, deeper leadership, stronger controls, clearer authority, more documentation, more discipline, and a willingness to let other people carry real responsibility. It is not built by accident, and it is not built quickly (as in a year or two). The original founder(s) will need to make some sacrifices in exchange for the returns offered from this potentially larger, stronger, more valuable business.

This path also requires a different mindset. The founder must gradually move knowledge, decision- making, accountability, and ownership capacity into the business itself. That is how independence is built. Not all at once, and not perfectly, but deliberately and over time. This path offers the greatest potential freedom and transferable value, but it asks the founder to change the most in return. In the end, this is the path I took.

The tradeoffs are real. Each of these paths has strengths. Each also has limits. The founder-dependent path offers control, identity, and simplicity, but usually at the cost of time, scalability, and transferable value. The middle path offers relief, resilience, and a stronger business without requiring total reinvention. The fully founder-independent path offers the greatest long-term freedom and value, but demands the most change, the most patience, and the greatest willingness to stop being the center of everything.

None of this is moral. It is structural.

You are not a better person because you choose one path over another. And you are not less impressive as an owner or founder because you choose a business that fits your temperament, priorities, and life. The point is not to impress anyone, or everyone. The point is to be honest about why you started a small business, what you are building, what it requires from you, and what it can realistically give back.

What you shouldn't do is hope for the third outcome or pathway, while continuing to operate entirely in the first or second business model or pathway.

Before we get to the build process – the Five-Year Plan – there is one more issue worth thinking about carefully... even after founders see the founder-dependent structure clearly and understand their options, many still stay exactly where they are on the treadmill, which is path one, for better or worse.

Why? Answering that question is where we go next.

★ ★ ★ ★ ★

CHAPTER FIVE

Why We Stay On The Treadmill

The vast majority of founders don't stay on their treadmill because they don't want to improve, or are not interested in growing larger or more valuable. They stay because the reasons for doing so sound completely logical, especially when the business is already demanding nearly everything they have. Many of those reasons reflect real constraints in time, money, and personnel. Others are familiar ways of thinking that helped us survive, grow, and succeed in the early years.

So, if you've ever thought or said any of the following, you're in very good company:

- I don't have time for anything more. I'm already overloaded.

- I'm great at what I do... and I can't find anyone else who will do it to my standard.

- I'm solely responsible for my success and I like it that way.

- My business is big enough. I'm not trying to build an empire.

- I'm competent, committed, and working hard. I can't do any more.

- I've made it this far. I'll make it to the end.

- No one will ever care more about this business than I do.

- I'm different. These ideas might work for others, but not for me.

- I can't afford the cost, or the risk, of letting go and changing things.

If one or more of these hit home, I am not here to shame you. Excuses or not, I have said most of them myself, more than once. Being a small business owner is a full-time job, and then some. The question is not whether your reasons are understandable, or even completely correct. The better question is whether they are still serving you, your goals, and the kind of business you actually want to build.

Many of these reasons are really signals, and they are worth listening to carefully. They may be clues that the business is still organized around you rather than around a repeatable, durable structure. If you hear yourself saying, "I can't delegate," the signal may be, "I don't yet have standards in place." If you're thinking, "No one can do it like me," the signal may be, "I don't yet have training, documentation, or checkpoints." These are not character flaws. They are structural problems, and structural problems can be solved, if you want them to be.

For some founders, those signals point not toward major change, but toward an honest and informed conclusion: the treadmill is exactly where they belong. Having control of everything is working. It is comfortable. It provides a good income and a good life. That is a legitimate and respectable outcome.

But for the founder whose reasoning is rooted mostly in fear, habit, exhaustion, or the belief that no one else can do what they do, those thoughts are worth examining more closely. What feels protective in the short run can quietly keep you stuck in the long run. This chapter is not intended to argue you out of your reasons. What I hope it will do is help you separate what is true or convenient from what is fear, and what is a real constraint from what is a solvable system problem. That clarity is what allows you to choose deliberately, whichever path you ultimately prefer.

As for finding the time... you'll have to make it happen deliberately. Start small, progress gradually, but do not procrastinate – too many other matters will step in front of you. Whatever your chosen path, pick it deliberately with due thought, and then move forward.

And if you don't know where to start, the Upgrades in the Five-Year Plan will guide you through the specific steps involved in building something stronger, something better. I find that it helps me to have a clear, linear plan of action, though I fully concede that you can take more or less than five years to get all this done, and you can re-order the entire Plan to fit your needs and preferences.

One last observation. I have often sat in conversations with a founder who wants a more independent business model, only to discover that their accountant, attorney, or financial advisor is also running on their own treadmill. People tend to surround themselves with others who think and act similarly. That is human nature. But it can also make it harder to see better alternatives. If the people around you have never built beyond a founder-dependent model, they may not be the best guides or support team for the improvements you are now considering. Growth and change sometimes require stepping outside the echo chamber.

You have already done the hardest part. You built something from nothing. You made payroll when it was difficult, served clients when you were exhausted, and kept going when the smarter bet, statistically speaking, was to stop. If a better future could be built board by board, decision by decision, it would look like a founder refusing to stop at survival. That is the foundation of success.

Now we build on it, not by tearing down what you've created, but by strengthening it, one Upgrade at a time, spaced over about five years. No grand, sudden reinvention. No dramatic leap. Just a sequence of practical moves that shift the weight of the business off of you, or mostly off of you, and into a structure that can carry it, as you continue to make a good living.

You've spent years working on your business. Now let's build it into something that can work better for you.

* * * * *

A Five-Year Plan
For Building A
Durable Business

The first part of this field guide was about seeing the treadmill clearly: how it forms, why it persists, and what paths are available to you. This next part is about building differently, and more purposefully. This is where the real work begins, and the results begin to take shape. If durability in business is something you can build, it is built one deliberate change at a time.

The Upgrades that follow are not meant to feel like a sudden pile of obligations. They are a sequence of practical structural improvements designed to help you make your business stronger, more durable, and less dependent on you over time, to the degree you choose. You may not need all of them, and you may have already done several on your own. And you can also take ten years to complete the list if you like!

But let's be clear about one thing. Small businesses are not simple to operate, at least not if you want something that produces a good, consistent living, is profitable, and holds real value over time. In today's world, durability requires more than hustle and good intentions. It requires structure, discipline, and a willingness to build on purpose. And building anything takes effort over a period of time. I'm here to help you with that as much as I can.

If you are leaning toward Path Two, the middle ground described in Chapter Four (i.e., less founder dependent), I would encourage you to focus first on Upgrades 2 through 5, at your chosen pace. For many founders, these four changes alone can make a small business meaningfully stronger, less fragile, and easier to own and operate.

One final note, you'll notice that the Upgrades are written in a very uniform manner. You might read them all in order, but I suspect most founders will implement them out of order and sometimes over more than five years. The goal is that whenever you decide to implement the next Upgrade, the presentation of the material will always feel familiar to you.

Year One
Build The Foundation

Year One is about creating a foundation your business can build on. These first three Upgrades establish clarity, legal and tax structure, and cash-flow control. Everything that follows becomes easier if you build this foundation well.

The Five-Year Plan that follows is presented in its fullest form. That is not because every founder should pursue full founder-independence and implement all fifteen Upgrades. It is because Path Three includes the widest range of structural improvements (all or most of which are required to support this choice), while Path Two simply requires fewer of them to achieve the result most founders actually want. In other words, I am showing you the complete build, not prescribing the same destination for everyone.

UPGRADE NO. 1
Get Specific About What You Want

Why it matters:

- The treadmill thrives on vagueness

- You can't build what you can't describe

- This is the foundation for every other Upgrade

- Your business should serve your life, not consume it

Let's start the business-building process by dreaming a little. Then we'll get specific and make things happen. A clear picture turns "someday" into something you can execute starting now, and *specific goals* prevent you from accidentally building a larger version of the same job. Entity structure, cash-flow systems, hiring, controls – none of them works well without a destination in mind.

Picture your business five years from now. The treadmill has been donated to a local charity. **Your business has doubled in gross annual revenue.** You're standing on your own two feet, not as the person who does everything, but as the leader of a growing, profitable, valuable small business. **You are the CEO.** It's your business and your dream, so what does that actually look like?

Get specific and write down answers as to:

- **Your Ideal Client Profile (ICP):** the type of client or customer your business is best built to serve– profitably, consistently, and with the least unnecessary complexity.

- **Your specific profitability target:** 15%, 20%, 25% (pick a relevant number appropriate to your line of work or your profession)

- **Your annual base salary:** what you will pay yourself as leader/CEO

- **Your ideal weekly schedule:** what your calendar looks like when the business isn't routed

- through you; include vacation time and think time away from the office

- **Your "Stop Doing" list:** the work you will no longer touch

- **Your surrounding/supporting talent:** help vs. capacity vs. outsourced

- **The investments required as to:** people, systems, tools, marketing

- **Balance-sheet strength:** cash on hand, reserves, assets, intellectual property

- **Your annual growth rate:** the pace you can sustain without impeding quality, culture, or margin

The idea is that when you know what matters, you delegate sooner, invest smarter, and stop chasing distractions. That said, start with your ICP, because **focus is leverage.** One of the most common reasons founders stay on the treadmill too long is that they try to serve too many kinds of customers in too many ways. That creates complexity, exceptions, and constant customization, which are exactly the conditions that force everything back through the founder.

A clear ICP is not a marketing exercise. It's an operating decision. When you decide who you serve (and who you politely don't), you simplify everything that follows: pricing, processes, hiring, delegation, quality control, and profitability. Write it out and adjust the profile over time.

A simple but powerful rule for Year One is this: **Learn to say "No" and say it often** as you reshape and strengthen your business. Saying "No" is how you protect capacity for the right clients, the right work, and the right growth. You can always change your mind later if you get it wrong or outgrow you past decisions.

The "CEO schedule" reality check. As you define your ideal weekly schedule, make sure it reflects the role you're trying to grow into. In a founder-independent business, the CEO's time should be spent primarily on:

- Systems and accountability

- Strategy, priorities, and growth

- People and leadership development

- Financial decisions and capital discipline

- Client and supplier relationships that truly matter in the long term

This is how you build a business that grows without consuming you. Keep in mind that these are goals for a business that will already be very different and, one day in the hopefully near future, about twice the current revenue level (*Build the Growth Engine* is Upgrade No. 10).

Think about that… In a business twice your current size, who will you need on your team? What specific talent will it take to serve and retain your ICP at that time? How will you find and retain that talent? Who on your team will be responsible for interviewing, hiring, and training that high-level talent? How will this approach affect your budget, your margin, and your forecasted growth rates? The point is to build out this business before you need it, because tomorrow will be here in the blink of an eye.

Finally, treat all of these thoughts as part of a living document. Draft it now. Revisit it in a quiet moment. Revise, as necessary. If you can see the future clearly enough to describe it, you can build it deliberately.

But whatever you decide, get specific and write it down.

* * * * *

UPGRADE NO. 2
Set Up The Proper
Entity And Tax Structure

Why it matters:

- Durability

- Risk containment

- Financial organization and tax efficiency

- Organizational clarity, continuity, and transferability

Think of your entity and tax structure as the concrete foundation under the business you are building. In one way or another, everything you build from this point forward attaches to, or relies on, this primary element. I don't mean this as an excuse, but there are entire books written on this subject. I'll present the important basics to consider in a couple of pages in this field guide, and provide you with some instructions to learn more if you'd like…

The first and most important lesson is that strong, valuable, transferable businesses require an entity structure. A sole proprietorship is, by design, a one-generation model. It isn't built to last. It usually ends with the founder, whether by retirement, disability, burnout, or a planned wind-down. It's also generally not investable, and rarely valuable beyond the income it produces. Its virtues are real, to be sure: speed, and simplicity. But it comes with significant structural limits.

So, what kind of entity structure should you use? The final answer depends on your location and any rules that apply to your profession. But a common and wise starting point is an **S-corporation**. Another strong option, especially for certain professional services firms or larger multi-owner businesses, is an **LLC taxed as a partnership**. Let's start to explore the LLC path as it is not only very flexible, it can also be very confusing until you know how it works. A basic, or what I call a *garden variety* S-corporation, is the simplest entity structure to work with. An LLC is the most sophisticated. It depends on what you're building.

A Limited Liability Company, or LLC, is a great first choice, but for some interesting reasons, it is often another way to structure your business as an S-corporation. Let me explain. With just one filing of your Articles of Organization, usually with your Secretary of State, the founding owner (or owners as a group) can choose to have the LLC taxed in one of the following four ways:

1) a DE, or disregarded entity (if there is only one owner)

2) a Partnership (if there are two or more owners)

3) a C-corporation, or

4) an S-corporation

Even better, these choices, or tax elections as they're commonly referred to, can be changed as your business grows. It is common, for example, to start your business as an LLC/DE, then migrate to a Partnership when a second owner buys in, and then progress to an LLC/S-corporation to take advantage of tax savings in many locations. In this regard, an LLC has no peer. It can adapt to your changing needs.

The common thread is that the choices I listed are all pass-through entities, meaning the business itself generally isn't taxed as a separate taxpayer at the federal level; profits pass through to owners and are taxed on each owner's individual returns pro rata, depending on the structure. More importantly, the next Upgrade (No. 3) will help you focus on isolating and maximizing your profits, or your bottom line as it is often called. Profits have a major impact on business value, can be distributed at a lower tax rate, and are often one of the key reasons next generation talent chooses to buy in when offered the opportunity. Profits are essential in a small business, but usually only in a tax conduit where they are distributed pro rata on a regular basis to the equity owners. The next Upgrade will be telling in this respect.

A C-corporation, by contrast, directly or as an LLC tax election is rarely the best choice for most small business owners, though there are exceptions and your advisor can help you evaluate them.

A key practical benefit of forming an entity is that it forces a financial separation of personal and business assets, cash flows, and expenses. To this end, and at a minimum, open a business checking account and a business savings/money market account in your entity's name. If your business qualifies, or as soon as it does, consider adding a business line of credit. These accounts serve to physically separate business cash flow from personal income. This level of formality is always better with a formal entity structure. With a good bookkeeper, such separation also creates clarity and discipline in your record keeping.

Another major benefit is limited liability. It's not a perfect shield, but it is meaningful especially when you avoid commingling business and personal assets and you treat the entity like a real business. An LLC/DE, for example, is treated by the IRS as a sole proprietorship, but through the LLC, it is a sole proprietorship with limited liability. That is important, even if you're a force of one.

The proper entity structure can also create tax efficiencies. For example, an S-corporation structure supports a W-2 compensation system for employees as well as owners/shareholders. A formal payroll (which can be outsourced) helps separate wages from profits and, in many cases, can reduce the tax burden on your profit distributions, depending on your facts and your advisor's guidance. Mind you, managing a payroll, even if just for one or two people, can be challenging so you'll want to coordinate this process with your accountant and a good payroll service. And be mindful that some cities, counties, and states in the U.S. have different rules and regulations as to the operation of an S-corporation. Still, I owned one for thirty years and I never regretted it. It saved me more, sometimes far more, than it cost in administrative fees.

Finally, an entity structure supports an **equity-centric** business, not just a founder-centric one. In a founder-centric or founder-dependent business, next generation ownership candidates (perhaps your son or daughter) are essentially investing in *you*. In an equity-centric business, key employees or family members can invest in a durable, professional system that produces cash flow, profitability, and value, independently of the founder. This is how succession planning works and how your business can outlive you, the topic of our final Upgrade, No. 15.

When you own or think in terms of a sole proprietorship, clients or customers become the medium of value. If you ever need or choose to sell your small business as a sole prop., the client list and related cash flow, along with any tangible assets, equate to your value. In an entity structure, the business "owns" the clients, cash flow, profits, and tangible assets. Stock, or equity, becomes the medium of value and stock can be sold incrementally such as 10% or 20% of the business entity. This is an important aspect of building duration into your business by retaining next gen talent who become investors AND employees.

Sit down with your CPA and attorney and talk through this step. It helps if they work with other businesses like yours because they can help you benchmark your growth and profit margins.

Most entities can be formed or setup at any time, but the cleanest timing is often the start of a calendar year or the start of a calendar quarter.

My best advice: don't delay on this Upgrade. This is the foundation that supports your goals and many of the Upgrades that follow. And if you've made a different choice, now you know what questions you should have asked! Please feel free to reach out to me with any questions through my author's website.

You can also learn more about these and other entity choices in my other books such as *Building With the End in Mind*, or *Acquiring Your Future...* both available at: www.davidgrausr.com.

* * * * *

UPGRADE NO. 3
Install A Professional Cash-Flow System

Why it matters:

- Profitability is emphasized and improved

- Key metrics become visible and trackable

- Higher profits support higher business value

- Owners get paid for the work/roles they perform

- Supports better planning for capital, hiring, and growth

Most small business owners manage cash flow very simply, by paying expenses first and then keeping what's left. I call this a **two-basket cash-flow system**: money comes in, bills get paid, and whatever remains is the owner's pay. It's common, and it can work for a long while. This approach supports and works well with treadmill thinking because high revenue *feels like* high profitability.

This Upgrade introduces a simple, powerful shift towards running your business like a business, not like your personal piggy bank (respectfully). It's a professional cash-flow approach that fits any pass-through entity structure. Equally relevant, this is the point where you shift from gross revenue as a measure of your success to profitability.

Once your entity is set up, open your business bank accounts. From this moment forward, **all business revenue is deposited into the business's primary checking account**. This revenue belongs to the business, not to you personally, at least not yet. Next, compartmentalize this business revenue into three baskets, mentally at first, and then on a spreadsheet:

- **Basket No. 1: Operating expenses.** Everything needed to keep the business running (excluding the owner's wages).

- **Basket No. 2: Owner's wage/base salary.** Compensation for work owners actively perform.

- **Basket No. 3: Profits.** What remains after Baskets 1 and 2 are fully funded.

The goal of the three-basket cash flow system is to protect and improve the health of the business, separate wages from profits, and build long-term value. Basket No. 1 and Basket No. 2 acknowledge a basic truth: everyone, including the owner, must be paid for work they perform. Basket No. 3 acknowledges another truth: **not every dollar left after expenses is your salary.** You must find balance to build a valuable, durable, perhaps even investable business.

Think like an investor for a moment, because when you start a small business that's exactly what you are. Basket No. 3 is your **return on investment (ROI).** Every industry is different, but as a starting guideline, let's say you aim toward **25% profitability** as a target and adjust based on your reality (some businesses can only generate half that, others far more). The point isn't the perfect number; it's building a habit of running decisions through this profitability lens.

From this day forward, every dollar you spend, whether on hiring, pricing, tools, or equipment, should be considered as to its impact on profitability. One of the most useful habits you can develop is to spreadsheet your Profit & Loss Statement, identify your three-basket reality, and track it consistently from year to year. These numbers will become some of the most important "dashboard gauges" you will ever use as an owner.

Understand that this is a cash management framework, not a full accounting system. Every business will still have other important cash-flow demands to plan for, including taxes, debt service, capital reinvestment, reserves, and working capital needs. The point here is not to replace good accounting; it is to help owners clearly distinguish between operating costs, pay for work performed, and true profitability.

Basket No. 1 is often the most difficult to manage, but you need to know what normal is for your business by tracking your costs and benchmarking your business results if possible. Basket No. 2 is often the easiest to manage because you effectively set your salary. In the world of an S-corporation, there are often tax advantages to keeping owner wages "reasonable" and allowing more return to show up as profits. In the long run, Basket No. 3, profitability, becomes one of the primary drivers of business value.

A quick example to close out this explanation: if your small business generates $1,000,000/year in gross revenue and you bring 25% to the bottom line of your P&L, then after Basket Nos. 1 and 2 are satisfied, $250,000 flows into the remaining basket as profits. In most cases, and as a matter of law in an S-corporation or LLC/S-corporation, profits (or losses) flow to each owner pro rata. These profit dollars may be paid out to you as an owner as your ROI, often quarterly, or they may be partially reinvested to help grow your business. The key is to understand that wages and profits are different things, paid out differently, and often taxed differently.

If your overhead (Basket No. 1) is 50% of your gross revenues, and you decide that your compensation should be $250,000/year as CEO, then this is a 50%/25%/25% cash flow system. If you are able to gradually reduce your overhead to 40% of gross revenue over the next five years through added efficiencies and cost cutting, and you reduce your salary to 20% over the same period as a percent of gross revenue, then you can operate a 40%/20%/40% cash flow system. Why does this matter?

Let us count the ways! First, if you operate as an S-corporation or an LLC/S-corporation, your profit dollars may be subject to a lower tax rate than your wage dollars. **Taking money home more efficiently as your business grows and over the coming decades makes a real difference.** Second, a small business with 40% profitability and that is no longer founder-dependent starts to build real value. Finally, the only way to access the dollars in Basket No. 3, which are now significant in this example, is to take the risk of ownership, something every founder has experienced. Increasing the amount and percentage of dollars flowing through Basket No. 3 is what makes a small business even more valuable, investable, and attractive to next gen talent. Don't fight to keep your best talent using only wages and bonuses–eventually use equity as the ultimate retention too and allow your key employee(s) to buy in.

Using a three-basket cash flow system to track your performance over time and to set goals for future growth and profitability is what differentiates a valuable business from owning a job.

$$\star\ \star\ \star\ \star\ \star$$

Using a three-basket cash flow system to track your performance over time and to set goals for future growth and profitability is what differentiates a valuable business from owning a job.

Build The Foundation
(Year One: Upgrades 1 Through 3)

Goal of Year One: Create clarity, legal and financial structure, and disciplined cash-flow management and visibility so the business has a stronger foundation for everything that follows.

Review cadence:

☐ Weekly (15 min)

☐ Monthly (30-45 min)

☐ Quarterly (60-90 min)

Date this checklist started: _______________________________

Target "Year One complete" date: ____________________________

UPGRADE NO. 1: Get Specific About What You Want

☐ I have a written five-year picture in plain language.

☐ I defined my Ideal Client Profile (ICP), including who we will not serve.

☐ I set measurable targets for profitability, compensation, growth, and balance-sheet strength.

☐ I defined my ideal weekly schedule as owner/CEO.

☐ I wrote a "Stop Doing" list and identified the top priorities on it.

☐ I identified the talent, tools, systems, and investments the business will eventually require.

Notes:

____

____

____

____

UPGRADE NO. 2: Set Up the Proper Entity and Tax Structure

☐ My entity structure has been reviewed and confirmed or upgraded with my CPA and/or attorney.

☐ My tax election is understood and intentionally chosen.

☐ Business checking and savings/money market accounts are open in the entity's name.

☐ Personal and business cash flow are clearly separated.

☐ Owner compensation approach is defined (salary, draw, distributions, or other appropriate structure).

☐ I understand the basic continuity, durability, and transferability benefits of the entity I chose.

Notes:

____

____

____

____

UPGRADE NO. 3: Install a Professional Cash-Flow System

☐ All business revenue is deposited into the business's primary checking account first.

☐ I am using the three-basket framework to separate operating expenses, owner wages, and profits.

☐ I review profitability, not just gross revenue, as a core measure of performance.

☐ I track my P&L consistently enough to understand my current three-basket reality.

☐ I am making spending decisions with their impact on profitability in mind.

☐ I am planning intentionally for taxes, reserves, debt service, reinvestment, and working capital needs.

Notes:

____

____

____

____

Year One "Proof of Progress"

Clarity of direction is:

☐ Vague

☐ Improving

☐ Clear

Entity/structure is:

☐ Unclear

☐ In progress

☐ In place

Cash-flow discipline is:

☐ Weak

☐ Improving

☐ Strong

Profit visibility and goals are:

☐ Low

☐ Better

☐ Consistent

Founder confidence in the plan is:

☐ Uncertain

☐ Growing

☐ Strong

Year One Reflection (10 minutes)

The most important thing we clarified this year:

____

____

____

The most important structural change we made:

____

____

____

The biggest remaining source of financial confusion:

____

____

____

The next focus for Year Two:

____

____

____

Printable *Action Guides* for each Year One Upgrade are available in the Resources section on my author's website at: https://davidgrausr.com/resources/.

* * * * *

Year Two
Create Stability

Year One gave you the basic foundation: direction, entity structure, and a more professional approach to cash flow, shifting the value proposition to profits rather than gross revenue. Year Two is about making the business more stable under real-world pressure, and building on top of the Year One Upgrades.

This is the year you begin reducing daily friction in a more visible way. You start documenting what only you know, buying back some of your time through a true leverage hire, and putting simple but essential controls in place so your business stops depending on your memory, your constant supervision, and your availability at every turn. If stability in business has a feeling, it is the quiet relief of no longer holding everything together by memory and force.

For many Path Two readers, Year Two will feel like the first year in which the business becomes meaningfully easier to own. As a reminder, focus on Upgrades 2, 3, 4, and 5, progressing at your chosen pace.

Printable *Action Guides* for each Upgrade in Year Two are available in the Resources section on my author's website at: https://davidgrausr.com/resources/

UPGRADE NO. 4

Get The Business Out of Your Head

Why it matters:

- Increases business value (supports predictable outcomes and cash flow)

- Consistency through written processes that produce repeatable outcomes

- Faster onboarding and training of future talent with less dependency on founder

The rule is simple: if it's important, write it down.

That rule and finding time to put words on paper, in detail, may feel overwhelming when you're still running hard just to keep everything moving. So, don't try to document everything all at once. Start with one strategic goal: document the work that currently requires your involvement. Then start to transfer it one piece at a time, sharing your knowledge, skills, and approach. If it's important, it must exist outside your brain in order to support your business goals.

As a founder, you are likely the smartest and most experienced person in the room every day. The best way to lift everyone else up to an adequate support level is to share what you know, what you expect, and how you do it, in writing. Writing it down doesn't make it permanent. Writings can be changed to adapt to the reality of the business and its clients or customers, and the employees you've hired to help you. Just remember that your words, wisdom, and experience on paper are the pathway to efficiency, consistency, and growing founder-independence. This is where you start to get your time back.

Don't aim for perfection. Aim for visibility. Once your process exists on paper, you can gradually begin to lead from a CEO's point of view, at least on that one issue, instead of working from the trenches with a poor view of the business field. Better yet, when team members follow your written processes, you will quickly see what works, what doesn't, and what should be improved. Expect to write and rewrite your Business Systems Manual over time. Constant improvement isn't a flaw in the process. IT IS THE PROCESS.

Try to capture the work flows, your applicable knowledge and management approach, while you're doing the work, or immediately afterwards, if possible. Don't rely on memory if you can avoid it. Yes, this will make you busier at first, but every process you document and successfully hand off buys back that time. That extra time becomes fuel for the next handoff. This compounding effect is one of the fastest ways off the treadmill, or to take control and onto a strong, durable business platform. I'll say it more than once because you need to hear it. Find the time.

Carry a pen and notepad for quick capture; details count. Then, once a day, transfer your notes into a single document titled: "How We Do Things." For each recurring task, create a short page using this template or a version adapted to your business:

- Purpose (why it exists or happens)

- Trigger (when it happens)

- Steps (5 to 10 bullet points)

- Standard (what *done right* looks like)

- Owner (who is responsible, or will be responsible)

- Time (typical time to complete the task)

- Tools/Templates (links or files used)

In terms of where to start, document the work that currently **requires You, but could be delegated.** Of course, if you're founder-dependent, it will feel like "everything" depends on you. That's normal. So start with this priority list and adapt it to your business:

1) Customer-facing promises (what you promise, what "good" looks like, and what you never compromise on)

2) Delivery steps (the workflow, tools, checkpoints, and standards that produce the result)

3) Exceptions (what to do when things go wrong, i.e., refunds, rework, escalations, edge cases)

4) Money (pricing, billing, collections, approvals, and cash-flow rules)

5) People (roles, decision rights, handoffs, and accountability).

This doesn't need to be fancy. It needs to be usable. Again, if it doesn't work in the hands of your team like it does in your mind, adjust the process for the reality of your situation. In the near future, when you not only hire the right people to perform these specific tasks, and authorize them to do so, they will improve on the instructions and processes you have provided. Let them! That's real ownership of the work.

A business is founder-independent, or more independent, when you can say, "This is how we do it here," and someone else can step in and make it happen.

* * * * *

Make Your First Leverage Hire

Why it matters:

- Reduced key-person risk

- Buys back the founder's hours every week

- A documented process isn't real until someone else can execute it

- A business that can perform without the founder's constant intervention is more durable, transferable, and valuable

When you can afford it, and after you've made real progress on the first four Upgrades, start assembling your team. Early on, you'll hire help to buy back time and to help your systems become real.

From personal experience, this is often the hardest Upgrade to execute well, so accept that this will take some practice and some time. Unlike setting up an entity structure or realigning your cash flow system, hiring is subjective. It involves judgment, uncertainty, and risk — and that's where many founders get stuck. Understand that getting it wrong occasionally is not a reason not to figure this out, even through trial and error. Sometimes, that is a good way to learn.

Common hiring hurdles: Finding the right person on a small-business budget is rarely easy. The best candidates often already have good jobs, and the wrong hire can cost you time, money, momentum, and confidence. On top of that, hiring does not create leverage on day one. You still have to define the role clearly, interview thoughtfully, onboard well, and stay engaged long enough for the person to become useful. And then that person needs to stay with your business long enough to make real progress and to own the work that they do. That is why many founders delay this Upgrade, until they are *more ready*. The risk is real, but so is the cost of remaining the bottleneck forever. You have to push through this step to make real progress, no matter how long it takes.

One common mistake is predictable – and thus avoidable: we tend to hire in our own image. We hire people who feel familiar, who think like us, work like us, and solve problems like us. It feels safe. It seems logical. You think you know what you're getting, more or less. The problem is that this approach won't get you off the treadmill or slow it down much. It just adds another version of you, at best, or someone you can train to be more like you, to the mix.

What you really need in the first five years, or so, of this process is a counterweight: someone who is strong where you are weak, who can take on meaningful work, and who can run the systems you are documenting. Start by writing a simple "Stop Doing This" list (perhaps in conjunction with Upgrade No. 4) of roughly ten things you must hand off within the next year. Then hire for that outcome. If the role and the person don't subtract meaningful work from you, slow down and rethink what you're doing. Hiring for "help" is too generic, too easy, and too inefficient. Make this hire really count.

Trust requires structure. Give a capable person a clear outcome, decision authority within reasonable bounds, and a simple reporting cadence to work with. If you hire someone but keep all decisions, approvals, and information running through you, you haven't hired leverage; you've hired a messenger, and you remain the gatekeeper. A more founder-independent business is built when responsibility and authority travel together. Hire the skills to own and perform specific tasks and then hold them to it.

Let's pause here for a moment and define a term you'll see throughout this field guide: **leverage.** Leverage is anything that reliably gives you time back by moving work, decisions, and follow-through from you, individually as the founder, into a system someone else can run. Leverage is time returned and dependency reduced.

When making a leverage hire, aim for outcomes, not traits. Early in my career, my overarching goal when I also tried to wear the Human Resources hat, was to hire "a hard worker" or "a trustworthy person," and I learned how unreliable that goal or standard is after a couple of interviews and subsequent hires. Sometimes I got lucky, but usually I didn't. What worked better was hiring for ownership of specific tasks or a specific role: "someone who can own billing and collections with minimal supervision," or "someone who can own client follow-up end-to-end."

One of the best approaches I was taught is to interview for proof, not promises. Ask for specific examples, not opinions. For example: "Tell me about a time you took a messy process, fixed it, and then made it repeatable." Good general follow-up questions might include: What did you change? What did you measure? What would you do differently next time? What does good customer service mean to you? How would you do it better?

For most founder-dependent businesses, your first true leverage hire is not a rainmaker or a "mini-me." More often, it is someone who brings operational execution or financial discipline to the business. In practical terms, that usually means one of two people:

- **An admin/operations lead** who keeps work moving and prevents routine tasks, follow-up, and coordination from routing back through you.

- **A bookkeeper or financially disciplined support person** who brings order to the numbers, improves visibility, and helps keep cash-flow discipline from depending entirely on the founder.

Either way, the standard is simple: this person should pay you back in the only currency that matters at this stage – meaningful hours returned to you each week. If the role does not create leverage, it is probably just overhead.

One more point for the 21st-century business owner: your first leverage hire does not always need to be a W-2 employee. In many businesses, the fastest path to leverage is outsourcing a specific function to a capable specialist or service provider such as bookkeeping, payroll, IT support, marketing execution, a fractional officer, or even a virtual assistant for scheduling and follow-up. That can be a smart Year Two, Year Three bridge because it buys back founder time without the full cost, complexity, and long-term commitment of payroll. It is also easier to unwind if the fit is wrong.

But whether the help is internal or external, leverage only works when expectations are clear, outcomes are measured, and accountability is real. Otherwise, the founder simply trades one kind of overload for another. That is why the next Upgrade matters so much.

Leverage without accountability, does not remain leverage for very long.

* * * * *

Install Simple Controls And Accountability

Why it matters:

- Creates leverage

- Increases business value

- Stops expensive surprises

- Supports consistent, dependable operations

- Prevents the founder from becoming the safety-net

In a small business, controls aren't bureaucracy. They're guardrails.

Controls and accountability let you step back without losing visibility or compromising on standards. They are the rules, ownership assignments, metrics, and routines that prevent mistakes, cash leaks, and avoidable surprises, while allowing your business to run without your constant supervision. Think in terms of providing specific answers to these questions:

- Who owns each recurring function (billing, onboarding, payroll, client follow-up)?

- What does "done right" look like?

- What gets reviewed weekly or monthly?

- Who approves spending, and under what thresholds?

- What gets reconciled every month (cash, receivables, payables)?

- What gets tracked (a basic key performance indicator, or KPI dashboard)?

- What happens when something is off?

Most small business pain comes from things that, in hindsight, you probably *should* have seen coming: cash shortfalls, missed deadlines, quality slips, client churn, compliance errors. Controls make problems visible early when fixes are still inexpensive and manageable.

Controls also replace founder supervision. Without clear ownership and check-ins, everything routes back to you. With such controls, responsibility and authority can travel together, and outcomes can be measured. That's where delegation becomes real and effective.

Consider installing controls in these five places first, one at a time:

1) **Ownership** (Who owns what in terms of tasks and functions?)

2) **Authority** (What can your team decide without you?)

3) **Thresholds** (What limits or approvals apply?)

4) **Reconciliations** (What must be checked regularly to avoid surprises?)

5) **Rhythm** (When and how often do we review and correct?)

These do not need to be fancy. They need to be clear, visible, and applied consistently. If any one of these is missing, founder-dependence creeps back in. Let's break each one down to give you a better understanding of what's involved and what to expect.

STEP 1: ASSIGN OWNERSHIP. ONE NAME PER FUNCTION. Founder-dependent businesses often rely on the mantra "everyone helps with everything." That sounds collaborative, but it is just as likely to create confusion and missed handoffs. Your first control is clarity. Assign a single owner to each recurring function (even if they delegate pieces of the process):

- Sales/intake owner

- Client service/delivery owner

- Money owner (billing, collections, payables, bookkeeping coordination)

- Operations owner (scheduling, workflows, documentation)

- Risk/compliance owner (as applicable)

If you're solo, or you only have one or two employees, your name will appear next to a lot of boxes at first. That's normal. At this point, this is about accountability, not headcount. In fact, seeing your name everywhere is useful: it shows you, in black and white, where the business is routing through you. That becomes your delegation roadmap. Make leverage hires to address this situation over time as your revenue and growth allow.

Rule: If it matters, it must have an owner.

Reality: Early on, that owner may be you.

STEP 2: CREATE DECISION RIGHTS. Founders often delegate tasks but keep all the decisions. That isn't delegation of authority. It's a longer to-do list. To address this, create *three lanes*:

- **Decide:** Team members can decide and act

- **Recommend:** Team member recommends; you approve

- **Inform:** Team members act, then keep you informed of what they did

Examples:

- Refunds up to $_________________ (Decide)

- Discounts beyond __________% (Recommend)

- Purchases under $___________ (Decide)

- Hiring/termination (Recommend)

- Client escalation: Inform (routine)/Recommend (exceptions)

This reduces interruptions and prevents routing back to you on every matter. If you don't have the people in place yet to take on real ownership, or you're not ready to grant authority to the people you have, revisit **Upgrade No. 5**, and gradually hire with these specific goals in mind.

STEP 3: PUT THE LIMITS IN WRITING. You don't need a policy manual. You need two or three numbers on one page that stops chaos:

- Spending approval threshold: $________________________
- Contract/signature authority (who signs what?)
- Pricing/discount thresholds: **% / $**________________
- Client exceptions (what qualifies, who approves?)

These controls protect your margin and help to prevent "But, I thought it would be OK…"

STEP 4: RECONCILIATIONS (THE "NO SURPRISES" DISCIPLINE). Reconciliations are not accounting trivia. They are how owners stay out of trouble. Trust matters, but verification protects everyone. **Hope is not a control.** Minimum reconciliations should include:

- Cash reconciled monthly (checking + money market + Line of Credit)

- Receivables reviewed monthly (who owes you what, for how long, remediation steps?)

- Payables reviewed monthly (what's coming due?)

- Payroll + tax set-asides confirmed monthly

Start there. Your business will become calmer immediately. Evolve this list to fit your business needs.

STEP 5: INSTALL THE PROPER CADENCE (THE HEARTBEAT OF ACCOUNTABILITY). Accountability doesn't come from personality, passion, caring, or lack of trust. It comes from rhythm. Start with two meetings:

Weekly (30 minutes): priorities + bottlenecks + commitments

- What are the top 3 priorities this week?

- What's stuck?

- Who owns what (by the next meeting)?

Monthly (60 minutes): scoreboard + cash + improvements

- What happened in the numbers?

- What broke or slipped?

- What do we fix next?

Controls and accountability are not about mistrust of your team and the owners of the various tasks and functions. They're about clarity and expectations. This is about replacing founder anxiety with verification so you can delegate without guessing, trust without hoping, and lead without hovering.

By the end of Year Two, your business should feel stronger, clearer, and at least a little less dependent on you. Year Three is where you begin turning these early improvements into something more consistent and repeatable. This is where shared standards, measurable results, and a more professional way of operating start replacing founder instinct and effort as the primary force holding the business together.

That is where we go next.

* * * * *

Create Stability
(Year Two: Upgrades 4 Through 6)

Goal of Year Two: Reduce daily friction by documenting critical knowledge, buying back founder time through leverage, and installing simple but essential controls so the business becomes more stable under real-world pressure.

Review cadence:

☐ Weekly (15 min)

☐ Monthly (30–45 min)

☐ Quarterly (60–90 min)

Date this checklist started: _______________________________

Target "Year Two complete" date: ___________________________

UPGRADE NO. 4: Get the Business Out of Your Head

☐ A shared "How We Do Things" document or manual exists.

☐ I am documenting work that can be delegated that currently requires my involvement.

☐ At least several core recurring processes are written down in usable form.

☐ Key customer-facing promises, delivery steps, exceptions, money rules, and people responsibilities are being documented.

☐ My written processes are being tested, improved, and used by others where appropriate.

☐ At least one important task or process now exists outside my head in a way someone else can follow.

Notes:

____

____

____

____

UPGRADE NO. 5: Make Your First Leverage Hire

☐ I created a "Stop Doing" list and identified the work I need to hand off.

☐ The role is designed around specific outcomes, not vague traits or generic "help."

☐ I understand how this role will buy back meaningful founder time each week.

☐ Decision authority for the role is clear enough for responsibility and authority to travel together.

☐ I considered whether the fastest path to leverage is a hire, an outsourced specialist, or fractional support.

☐ Founder time has measurably decreased in at least one meaningful area.

Notes:

____

____

____

____

UPGRADE NO. 6: Install Simple Controls and Accountability

- ☐ Every key recurring function has a named owner.

- ☐ Basic decision rights are clear (decide/recommend/inform).

- ☐ Spending, pricing, and exception thresholds are written down.

- ☐ Cash, receivables, payables, and payroll/tax set-asides are reviewed and reconciled regularly.

- ☐ A weekly check-in rhythm exists for priorities, bottlenecks, and commitments.

- ☐ A monthly review rhythm exists for numbers, issues, and improvements.

Notes:

____

____

____

____

Year Two "Proof of Progress"

Critical knowledge is:

- ☐ Still mostly in my head

- ☐ Partly documented

- ☐ Increasingly shared

Founder time bought back is:

- ☐ Minimal

- ☐ Some

- ☐ Meaningful weekly hours

Ownership and accountability are:

- ☐ Vague

- ☐ Improving

- ☐ Clear

Controls and visibility are:

- ☐ Weak

- ☐ Better

- ☐ Consistent

Business stability is:

- ☐ Fragile

- ☐ Improving

- ☐ Stronger under pressure

Year Two Reflection (10 minutes)

The most important thing we documented this year:

____

____

____

The most meaningful leverage we created:

____

____

____

The biggest remaining routing-back-through-me problem:

____

____

____

The next focus for Year Three:

____

____

____

Printable *Action Guides* for each Upgrade in Year Two are available in the Resources section on my author's website at: https://davidgrausr.com/resources/

* * * * *

Year Three
Build The Operating System

By Year Three, you should have a stronger foundation under your business: clearer goals, better legal and financial structure, more disciplined cash flow, core knowledge documented outside your head, a first leverage hire, and basic controls and accountability in place.

Year Three is where you begin turning that stronger foundation into a more consistent operating system. This is the year you rely less on memory, urgency, and constant founder intervention, and more on shared standards, clear direction, measurable results, and repeatable routines. If order in business has a sound, it is the quiet hum of people and systems working without needing the founder at every turn.

The Upgrades in Year Three work together to strengthen how the business operates day to day: your mission statement, your monthly scoreboard, and a more professional client service model. This is where the business begins to perform with greater consistency, not because the founder works less, but because the business itself starts working better.

Note that even if you do not plan to pursue full founder-independence, Year Three still matters. Shared direction, visible performance, and a more consistent client experience can make a founder-led business calmer, clearer, and easier to own. Path Two readers may not need to formalize every part of the operating system, but they will benefit greatly from reducing improvisation, inconsistency, and founder-only decision making. It is certainly worth considering!

UPGRADE NO. 7
Write Your Mission Statement

Why it matters:

- Installs your culture by design

- Provides clarity of business direction and purpose

- Improves speed of delivery (fewer "check with the founder" moments)

- Alignment through explicit standards (hiring, priorities, tradeoffs get easier)

Sooner than later, you must be able to articulate your direction, your purpose, and your non-negotiables. Then your staff must be able to do the same, from memory and almost intuitively. This Upgrade is how that process begins and, later, evolves. If you are not clear on what your business is trying to do, how it intends to do it, and what standards matter most, no one else can consistently make good decisions without your ongoing involvement.

That is especially important at this stage of the Five-Year Plan. By Year Three, you are no longer just building the foundation of the business. You are building its operating system. And operating systems need shared direction. If people don't know what matters, where the business is heading, and how decisions should be made, they will keep routing questions, uncertainty, and judgment calls back through the founder.

In a small business, culture forms whether you design it or not. Culture is not a slogan painted on a wall in the lobby. It is what actually happens every day: what you tolerate, what you reward, and how decisions get made under pressure, especially when no one is looking. In founder-dependent businesses, culture often becomes: "Do what the founder does," or worse, "Do what the founder wants today." That creates confusion, inconsistency, and dependency.

A mission statement does not create culture by itself. But it does give culture a written starting point. It puts into words what matters here, how you intend to operate, and what your team should be aiming to protect and deliver. Then hiring, training, accountability, and daily decisions reinforce those words until they begin to feel normal and shared.

Writing out your mission statement is how you begin replacing "follow me" with "follow our written standard." It is how you get your thinking out of your head and onto paper so your business is not guided only by founder instinct, memory, or mood. Over time, many businesses expand this into a mission, vision, and purpose statement. For a small business, these terms do not need to be complicated:

- **Mission** is what you do every day: who you serve, how you help, and the standard you intend to deliver.

- **Vision** is where you are heading: what you are trying to build over time.

- **Purpose** is why the business exists beyond simply making money: the deeper value you create for customers, employees, and the people you serve.

In a larger, often publicly traded company, these may appear as three separate polished statements. In a small business, one clear and usable statement is often better than three separate, coordinated statements that no one remembers. The goal is not wordsmithing. The goal is clarity. A good statement will not answer every question that arises, but it should point people in the right direction when you are not in the room.

Here are a few examples of how a small business might combine mission, vision, and purpose into one practical guiding statement:

For an independent coffee shop: We serve excellent coffee in a welcoming place where people can gather, connect, and feel at home, while supporting our community and sourcing responsibly.

For a financial advisor: We help families and business owners make wise financial decisions through clear advice, disciplined planning, and long-term thinking, so they can build security and protect what matters most.

For a residential real estate agent: We help buyers and sellers move with confidence through clear advice, strong communication, and honest guidance, so they can make good decisions at every stage of the process.

For a medical office: We provide timely, high-quality care with compassion, consistency, and respect, so every patient feels heard, helped, and treated well.

For a local bakery: We make healthy, handcrafted baked goods that nourish our community, support our team, and contribute to a stronger, more connected neighborhood.

These statements do not need to be perfect. They need to be usable. They need to be clear enough that someone on your team can make a better decision, when necessary and appropriate, guided by the overarching principles and standards of the business. The goal is that your team can explain your mission, vision, and purpose and apply it to daily activities without your constant oversight.

Here is my own combined mission, vision, and purpose statement:

I help owners build stronger, less founder-dependent businesses, prepare them for continuity and succession, and guide them toward becoming durable enterprises that make a real and lasting difference in the world.

What's yours?

* * * * *

Build A Monthly Scoreboard

Why it matters:

- Creates accountability

- Turns goals into a plan

- Visibility replaces anxiety

- Helps the founder lead by facts instead of stress or emotion

Year Three is about building the operating system. Upgrade No. 7 gives the business shared direction through a clear mission statement. Upgrade No. 8 adds the measurement layer, making performance visible and reviewable. Upgrade No. 9 then carries that work into the client experience, so the business delivers its standards more consistently and professionally.

Without a scoreboard, accountability becomes opinion, and values become slogans. With a scoreboard, you can see what is working, what is slipping, and what needs attention early, while fixes are still less expensive and less urgent. In short, Upgrade No. 8 is how you lead by facts instead of stress or emotion.

Setting up a scoreboard that works for you is not complicated, or at least it doesn't need to be. It can be as simple as a one-page overview of the key numbers that tell you how your business is performing and what you should be concerned about next. I started there twenty years ago, and over time we graduated to a spreadsheet that became more and more detailed as the business became larger. But I never forgot the value of those *one-page numbers* we had grown accustomed to tracking and watching. Think of this process like the gauges on a car. You do not need to be a mechanic to drive well or drive safely, but you do need to see the fuel level, speed indicator, and warning lights at a minimum.

Let's begin with the basics of what to measure. The universal rule is simple: **If it matters, measure it. If you measure it, review it. If you review it, act on it.**

Your initial scoreboard should include **10 to 15 key metrics**, grouped into four basic buckets:

1) **Money** (financial health)

2) **Customers/Clients** (demand and retention)

3) **Operations** (capacity and quality)

4) **People** (execution and bench strength)

These four groups will work for almost any small business. Start with the measures that make the most sense for your circumstances. If you are unsure, use this full list as your first draft and refine it over time. The goal is not to measure everything. The goal is to measure enough of the right things that you can see trouble early and make better decisions sooner. Tracking these items over time will help you better understand your business and what you can expect from it.

Money

- Revenue (monthly, quarterly, and year-to-date)

- Profit margin percentage (Basket No. 3 from Upgrade No. 3 in Year One)

- Cash on hand (and months of runway or reserves based on average expenditures)

- Accounts receivable (if applicable)

- Accounts payable

Customers/Clients

- Leads or opportunities created

- Conversion rate

- Average sale or project value

- Retention or repeat rate

Operations

- Work in progress or backlog

- Cycle time (how long work takes from start to finish)

- Rework, returns, or defects (quality control indicator)

People

- Staffing adequacy (are you over- or under-staffed?)

- A simple capacity indicator (weeks booked out, utilization percent, backlog, or WIP)

- One simple productivity measure (i.e., output per week or per person)

You do not need perfection or decimal places. You need a baseline. Once you begin tracking these measures consistently, you will add some, remove others, and shape the scoreboard to fit your business more precisely. Over time, the scoreboard also teaches your team what matters, because people pay attention to what is measured, reviewed, and discussed consistently.

Next, connect your monthly scoreboard to two other tools: **your forecast** and **spending plan.**

Your scoreboard tells you what happened and what is trending. Your forecast tells you where you're headed if nothing changes. Your spending plan, or budget, reflects the choices you make in response.

Forecasting does not require a finance degree. It is simple input/output math. Forecasting asks questions like these:

- What is our annual revenue goal?

- How many leads or opportunities do we need per quarter or per year?

- At what conversion rate?

- At what average sale or project value?

- At what margin?

- With what capacity to deliver?

Your spending plan is the process of assigning dollars to achieve your goals. It answers questions like:

- How much will we spend on marketing to generate the needed leads?

- What payroll can we support?

- How does this compare with last year's budget and growth rate?

- What tools, systems, or equipment should we buy this year?

- How much in cash reserves do we already have, and how much more do we need?

- What profit target are we trying to protect?

Once these basics are in place, develop good habits. Each month, update the scoreboard. Each month, compare it to the forecast. Each month, make small adjustments to the budget and priorities before the year gets away from you. That is how owner-operated businesses become owner-led businesses, and this is one of the most important benefits of becoming more founder-independent – time to address and think through these matters.

As you move toward a less founder-dependent model, treat the scoreboard as a shared discipline. If you have a leadership team, involve them. Schedule a monthly scoreboard meeting, usually sixty minutes, and review the numbers and trends together. As the founder, do as much listening as leading. Who came prepared? Who can interpret the facts, connect them to what is happening on the ground, and consistently recommend the right actions? What lies over the horizon in terms of threats or changing economic conditions?

To keep this from becoming "spreadsheet theater," end the meeting with three questions:

- What moved significantly on our scoreboard?

- Why?

- What will we do next month because of it?

If *nothing* changes as a result of the scoreboard review, the scoreboard isn't helping you. The goal is not reporting for the sake of reporting. The goal is better decisions, made earlier, with less guesswork and less drama. In the world of a small business, things are always changing-if you have time to pay attention. This is how you replace guesswork with leadership.

A scoreboard helps you see your business more clearly. The next question is whether the client experience itself is being delivered with the same level of clarity, consistency, and intention. That is where we go next.

* * * * *

Professionalize Your Client Service Model

Why it matters:

- Margins improve
- Business value increases
- Delegation becomes possible
- Standardization reduces chaos
- Consistency protects your good reputation

Most small businesses already serve customers or clients in a way that feels personal and flexible, and that is a real strength. But unchecked flexibility can also become a serious problem. Every custom promise creates a custom process, and every custom process is more expensive and more difficult to manage on a consistent basis.

In practical terms, every exception creates a new fire. Over time, the founder becomes the only person who can remember what was promised, how it is supposed to work, and what to do when something goes even slightly wrong. If you want less chaos, you need fewer unmanaged exceptions. And if you want fewer unmanaged exceptions, you need a clearer client service model. Welcome to Upgrade No. 9!

That doesn't mean the goal is zero exceptions. In a small, client-facing business, that premise is usually not even realistic, let alone desirable. Sometimes you simply need the ability to react and adapt quickly. But you also need the discipline to return to your standard model rather than reinventing the business for each customer or client.

A simple, professional, client service model answers these questions:

- What do you sell?

- Who do you sell it to?

- What do you promise?

- How do you deliver it?

- How do you handle exceptions?

- How do you keep it consistent?

This Upgrade is where you begin turning "but we do good work" into a repeatable, teachable, and more scalable service that your team can deliver without your constant involvement. For many small businesses, this feels uncomfortable at first. Standardization can sound cold, corporate, and/or overly rigid. But that is certainly not the goal(s). The goal is to make your service more predictable, more reliable, and easier for your team to deliver well. That is exactly what most clients want anyway.

Build a first draft in 30 minutes. Set a timer for 30 minutes and build a usable first draft. If it were me, I would grab a legal pad, but do it however you prefer. Do not aim for perfection. Aim for clarity. Write out your:

- **Core service offering (1 sentence):** What do we do, for whom, and what result do we deliver?

- **Top 5 deliverables:** What do clients or customers get from us reliably?

- **Onboarding process (10 steps max):** What happens from "yes" to first delivery?

- **Client or customer cadence:** How often do we meet, deliver, or check in, and what is included?

- **"Done-right" standards (3 rules):** What must always be true for quality control?

- **Top 5 exceptions:** What currently creates chaos? Which exceptions are truly necessary?

- **Tier differences:** What changes between Core and Premium in terms of speed, access, extras, or price?

Then refine it the next day. And again next month. The goal is not perfection. The goal is a service model that gets clearer, stronger, and more reliable over time.

A quick note on tiers. This is not about becoming corporate, and it is not about squeezing your customers or clients. Tiers are about controlling exceptions.

In many founder-dependent businesses, the founder creates premium access informally through special attention, faster turnaround, extra calls, and custom work, often without realizing it. The problem is not generosity. The problem is that these extras are often unpriced, undefined, and difficult for anyone else on the team to deliver consistently, let alone profitably. A tiered service model makes those differences explicit, correctly priced, and repeatable, so the relationship does not have to be renegotiated every time.

At a minimum, define two tiers:

- **Core:** your standard offer, standard turnaround time, standard access, and standard deliverables

- **Premium:** faster turnaround, more access, and/or additional deliverables, with clear boundaries and a clear price

Your tiers can differ on a few simple dimensions:

- **Speed** (turnaround time)

- **Access** (frequency or priority of calls, response time)

- **Scope** (what is included versus excluded)

- **Customization** (how much tailoring you allow)

- **Price** (the premium should fund the extra capacity required)

The goal is not to invent complexity, or to try to eliminate it. The goal is to contain it. Clients can then choose the level of service they want, and your team can deliver it without constantly creating one-off exceptions. In fact, many exceptions disappear the moment you turn them into a clearly defined premium tier.

Write down the specific rules for exceptions. As the founder, decide in advance and let your team know:

- What qualifies as an exception?

- Who can approve it? And who can say "No."

- How is it priced?

- How is it documented?

If something happens more than a few times a year, it is probably no longer an exception. It is part of the service model, and it should be defined, priced, and delivered accordingly. That is how a founder-dependent service model begins to turn into a professional one.

By the end of Year Three, the business should be operating with more clarity, more consistency, and less dependence on founder memory, improvisation, and constant intervention. You have put your directions into words, made performance more visible, and begun defining a client experience your team can actually deliver with greater consistency. And that matters because growth without consistency usually creates more chaos, not more freedom.

Year Four is where we begin building real carrying capacity. Once the business knows what it stands for, what to measure, and how to deliver its work more predictably and reliably, you are finally in a position to grow more deliberately, scale with systems, and add capacity without simply increasing the founder's burden.

That is Year Four of the plan.

* * * * *

Build The Operating System
(Year Three: Upgrades 7 Through 9)

Goal of Year Three: Build a more consistent operating system through shared direction, visible performance, and a more professional client service model, so the business works better without constant founder intervention.

Review cadence:

☐ Weekly (15 min)

☐ Monthly (30–45 min)

☐ Quarterly (60–90 min)

Date this checklist started: ________________________________

Target "Year Three complete" date: ____________________

UPGRADE NO. 7: Write Your Mission Statement

☐ Our mission, vision, and purpose are written in a clear and usable form.

☐ The statement is simple enough that key team members can explain it in their own words.

☐ Our standards and non-negotiables are clearer than they were before.

☐ The statement is being used to guide decisions, hiring, priorities, and tradeoffs.

☐ The business is less dependent on founder instinct, memory, or mood for everyday direction.

☐ We are beginning to build culture more intentionally, not accidentally.

Notes:

____

____

____

____

UPGRADE NO. 8: Build a Monthly Scoreboard

☐ We have a monthly scoreboard with a manageable set of key metrics.

☐ The scoreboard includes the main items/issues that matter in our business (money, customers/clients, operations, and people).

☐ We review the scoreboard on a set monthly basis.

☐ We connect the scoreboard to a forecast and a spending plan or budget.

☐ At least some decisions are now being made earlier because the numbers made an issue visible sooner.

☐ The scoreboard is helping us lead more by facts and less by stress, guesswork, or emotion.

Notes:

____

____

____

____

UPGRADE NO. 9: Professionalize Your Client Service Model

☐ We can describe our client or customer service model more clearly than before.

☐ Our core service offering, top deliverables, onboarding steps, and basic cadence are defined in writing.

☐ Our "done-right" standards are clearer and more teachable.

☐ We have identified recurring exceptions and are managing them more intentionally.

☐ We have clearer boundaries between standard service and premium or custom service.

☐ The client experience is becoming more consistent, teachable, and less founder-dependent.

Notes:

____

____

____

____

Year Three "Proof of Progress"

Shared direction is:

☐ Vague

☐ Improving

☐ Clear

Performance visibility is:

☐ Low

☐ Better

☐ Consistent

Client experience is:

☐ Founder-led

☐ More defined

☐ More consistent

Operating discipline is:

☐ Reactive

☐ Improving

☐ Reliable

Founder intervention in daily decisions is:

☐ Constant

☐ Reduced

☐ Meaningfully reduced

Year Three Reflection (10 minutes)

The most important standard we clarified this year:

____

____

____

The metric or trend that taught us the most:

____

____

____

The biggest remaining source of inconsistency:

____

____

____

The next focus for Year Four:

____

____

____

Printable *Action Guides* for each Upgrade in Year Three are available in the Resources section on my author's website at: https://davidgrausr.com/resources/

* * * * *

Year Four
Build Capacity & Authority

Year Four is where you begin converting a stronger operation into real carrying power.

This is the year you move beyond relief and into capacity. You'll work on growth in a more deliberate way, learn how to scale without adding chaos, and make your first true capacity hire so the business can produce more without requiring more of your time.

In addition, this is the year the question of authority comes into sharper focus. Capacity without authority creates frustration. Authority without standards creates risk. To build a business that can carry more weight without routing everything back through you, both must develop together.

For Path Two readers, Year Four is not about building a large enterprise for its own sake. It is about adding enough carrying capacity that growth, demand, and day-to-day pressure stop flowing entirely back through the founder. You may not need every element of this Year, but some combination of better growth discipline, stronger systems, and added capacity can make the business far more resilient and far less exhausting to own. Again, some ideas for you to consider now or in the future.

Build The Growth Engine

Why it matters:

- Growth prevents stagnation

- Growth funds independence

- Predictable growth reduces founder stress

- Consistent, strong growth improves valuation

By **Year Four**, the business should already be stronger, clearer, and more consistent than it was when you began. You have built a better foundation, installed necessary structure, and started defining how your business should actually operate. Now the question becomes whether it can grow consistently without pulling you back into the center of everything.

That is where the growth engine comes in.

A growth engine is not random marketing activity, occasional bursts of networking, or founder heroics whenever revenue feels tight or you have the time. It is a repeatable way to earn new revenue without depending on the founder to make it happen personally every week.

To be clear, top-line revenue growth is the subject of this Upgrade. The steady growth of your gross revenue, usually the top line of your Profit & Loss Statement, matters because it is the fuel that powers everything else in the business, including profits, hiring, reserves, owner compensation, value, and ultimately your freedom. Profits are still the ultimate scorekeeper, but steady top-line growth is often the clearest early sign that the business is gaining momentum and earning the right to invest in its future.

The goal is not growth for its own sake. It is growth that is profitable, visible, and durable enough to support the stronger business you are building.

Here is the practical point: founder-dependent businesses usually grow through founder effort. The owner sells. The owner markets. The owner networks. The owner makes things happen. That works in the early years, but it does not scale well, and it does not transfer well to a future buyer, successor, or investor.

A less founder-dependent business requires something different – growth that is repeatable, shared, and system-driven. It means a more consistent process for generating demand and converting that demand into paying customers, who are then served by trained and capable staff. In simple terms, you need two things:

- A steady inflow of qualified opportunities

- A consistent process for converting those opportunities into paying customers

If either one depends entirely on the founder, the treadmill is still running.

Choose one primary engine, then measure it. Most small businesses do best when they choose **one primary growth engine** and work it consistently before trying to add complexity. Common examples include:

- **Referrals** — deliberate and engineered, not merely hoped for

- **Authority/content** — consistent publishing, speaking, teaching, or video

- **Outbound/partnerships** — disciplined outreach and relationship building

- **Local discovery** — Google, maps, reviews, and local visibility

- **Paid advertising** — buying attention in a measured and intentional way

- **Retention and expansion** — repeat business, packages, memberships, upsells, and deeper client relationships

Pick one. Work on it every month. Measure it. Then improve it. At a minimum, use your scoreboard to track:

- Leads or opportunities created

- Conversion rate

- Average sale or project value

- Pipeline value

- Repeat rate or retention

- Gross margin (so growth does not quietly erode profitability)

When the pipeline is visible, you can stop guessing. When it is not, most founders substitute anxiety for clarity and default back to working harder.

Do not expect the first growth engine to work perfectly right away. Marketing and sales are learned disciplines. Failures, weak conversion, wasted effort, and false starts are part of the process. Think it through, adjust, and try again. In my own consulting business, guided by a professional marketing team, we eventually used almost all of these growth engines (except for local discovery, because ours was a national business). The point isn't to guess or hope your way into strong, consistent growth. The point is to build and refine a repeatable engine that fits your business model.

Once the first engine is producing useful data and reasonably reliable results, add a second one if appropriate; not before.

The founder should not remain the only engine of growth. At some point, many founders discover a hard but necessary truth: they should not remain the sole long-term engine of growth. Year Four may be the right time to invest in dedicated marketing or sales capability, whether internal, outsourced, or fractional, with clear goals and an appropriate budget. Taking this important step allows existing talent to do what it does best. I often explain this as allowing leaders to lead, marketers to market, and salespeople to sell.

This does not mean the founder disappears from growth; far from it. It means the founder stops being the only person responsible for making it happen.

A quick planning tool: the Rule of 70. One simple planning tool worth knowing is the **Rule of 70**. If you want to estimate how long it takes to double your revenue, divide 70 by your actual or targeted annual growth rate. For example:

- **10% growth** → about **7 years** to double

- **20% growth** → about **3.5 years** to double

This is not precise forecasting. It is a rough planning tool. But it is useful because it helps founders think more clearly about pace, patience, and the size of the opportunity in front of them. If your small business can grow consistently at 10% per year, then over the course of a twenty-year career it may grow to roughly six or seven times its original size. That is the quiet power of compounding.

But growth alone doesn't solve founder-dependence. If anything, unmanaged growth can make the treadmill steeper. If the business doubles in size but still relies on the founder to make the key decisions, solve the recurring problems, and carry the load, then the business has not really changed. It has only become larger and more demanding.

That is why growth must be matched by stronger systems. Once demand becomes more visible and more deliberate, the business has to learn how to carry that added weight without pulling the founder back into the center of everything.

That is why it is so important to learn how to grow your business in a scalable way.

* * * * *

UPGRADE NO. 11
Scale With Systems

Why it matters:

- Reduces fragility

- Improves margins

- Increases business value

- Makes growth sustainable

- Breaks the link between growth and founder hours

A note for Path Two readers: do this one Upgrade, or at least spend some time thinking it through. In this context, scaling does not mean building a much bigger company. It means reducing chaos, improving efficiency, and creating more value without dragging yourself back into the center of everything.

Let's get right to the point. People say "scale" when they mean "grow," and they are not the same thing.

Here is the cleanest version I can give you: to **scale** a small business is to increase output faster than you increase input. In plain English-the business grows, but you do not have to work proportionally harder to make it happen. If output still depends on founder hours worked, then the business may be growing, but it is not really scaling.

Some simple but important rules:

- If revenue doubles and your hours (or total work hours) double, that is growth

- If revenue doubles and your hours (or total work hours) stay roughly the same, that is scaling

- If revenue grows while margins improve and chaos decreases, that is healthy scaling — the kind that builds a stronger, more durable, more valuable business

Founder-led growth depends on constant hustle. Scaling depends on sound design. It requires systems that support delegation, repeatable processes, financial structure, and enough bench strength that the business can carry more weight without routing everything back through the founder.

And this takes us right back to the treadmill.

A founder-dependent business can grow for a while on sheer effort. But eventually the strategies that worked early stop working efficiently. You hit a wall. There is too much to do, not enough hours, and the founder becomes the constraint. The common response is to hire another *you* and keep doing what worked before. The result is predictable. The business may get bigger, but not better or stronger. Profitability stays flat or declines. Complexity increases. The treadmill speeds up.

Scalability is not optional if you want independence. If a business cannot grow without more founder time and effort, it is not truly scalable, and it's not very transferable. Your work may support your family and your lifestyle just fine. But if the business cannot grow without more founder time and effort, it is unlikely to look especially valuable to a buyer who thinks like an investor.

If you strip it all down, scaling requires five things:

1) **A standardized service model** — what you sell and how you deliver it

2) **Documented processes** — so quality is repeatable

3) **Clear roles and decision rights** — so work does not route back to you

4) **A scoreboard** — so you can lead by facts instead of stress

5) **One or more growth engines** — to support strong, consistent growth

The point of this Upgrade is not to build a massive company. The point is to build a business that can carry more weight efficiently and predictably, powered by better systems, better structure, and less founder dependence.

So let's take a practical approach and figure out how to scale without breaking your business or disrupting your income. Start by assuming the business can grow at a manageable pace. If you can sustain 10% annual growth, the business will roughly double in about seven years. That is not hype. It's math. And it's enough growth to fund better systems, better people, and better leverage over time. When you are ready, do this:

- **Define what must stay true as you grow.** What standards are non-negotiable? What do you refuse to compromise on?

- **Identify the next constraint.** Where does the real pressure point come from right now: lead generation, delivery capacity, founder approvals, cash flow, or something else? Pick one constraint and solve that next.

- **Build the system before you add volume.** Do not scale chaos. Standardize the service model. Tighten the processes. Clarify the handoffs. Then add volume.

- **Add talent that changes the trajectory.** In many small businesses, sales and marketing become the pinch point because the owner believes, "I'm the only one who can bring in revenue." That belief is common, but often incomplete and sometimes just plain wrong. Hiring or contracting for capable marketing and sales support, with clear goals and a practical budget, is often what turns growth from founder-powered to system-powered.

- **Scale for the business you are becoming.** As revenue grows over time, the business needs better systems, clearer roles, stronger discipline, and more carrying capacity. Don't wait until growth forces the change. Start planning now and build into that next version of the business gradually.

I would be doing you a disservice to make this process seem easy and/or inevitable. It's not. Scaling is difficult because it requires a different skill set than entrepreneurship. Early on, you solve problems with effort and willpower. That is often enough to survive. It's not enough to scale even as you gain experience as an owner. Scaling requires planning, design, systems, roles, metrics, and discipline. You will not master it by reading a few pages of suggestions and guidance, but you can get meaningfully better once you know what to look for and where to focus next.

The principle to remember is simple: scaling is not about getting bigger. Scaling is about becoming less dependent. You know you are scaling when the business grows and your role becomes more strategic, not more stressed.

But systems alone do not create capacity. At some point, the business also needs people who can carry real weight inside the structure you have built. Growth creates demand. Systems make that demand manageable. Capacity hires make it sustainable.

That's where we go next.

* * * * *

Make Your First Capacity Hire

Why it matters:

- Creates room for healthier growth

- Protects service quality as demand grows

- Reduces founder dependence in a meaningful way

- Builds the kind of structure buyers, successors, and investors value

- Increases output without increasing founder hours at the same rate

Path Two note: Optional, but useful if demand is outgrowing delivery.

In Chapter 3, we explored *the capacity illusion*, which is the belief that adding help automatically makes a business less founder dependent. It doesn't. Help can reduce stress in the short run, but if decisions still route back through the founder, the business has gained activity, not real capacity. Relief is useful. Capacity is what creates independence.

A capacity hire is different from finding someone to help you. A capacity hire is designed to own a defined slice of output, with clear standards, decision rights, and measurable outcomes. This supports your efforts to scale your business because production is no longer tied directly to the founder's personal bandwidth or number of hours worked.

This is also the moment Year Four stops being mainly about preparing for growth and starts becoming capable of carrying it.

Common hiring hurdles. Capacity hiring is one of the most important and difficult growth moves a founder makes. It takes an investment of time and money before the full return is visible, and the wrong hire can slow you down instead of freeing you up. Even the right person requires training, repetition, feedback, and time to reach full productivity.

That's why this Upgrade should follow proven demand, a clear role design, and a defined ramp to ownership of tasks and functions. Capacity is built deliberately, not wishfully. So before you hire, slow down and define the problem you are actually trying to solve. Capacity is not created by adding a person, or two. It is created by adding the right person, in the right place, for the right reason. Here is a simple five-step process for turning proven demand into real capacity.

Step 1: Determine where capacity is needed (don't guess). Capacity should be added where demand is already proven and measured. Identify the constraint. Look for signs such as:

- Backlog is growing

- Customers or clients are waiting too long

- Quality is slipping because the business is stretched

- The founder is still the only producer or rainmaker

- Good work is being delayed, declined, or rushed because capacity is already full

Pick one area where more output would directly improve throughput and protect standards. Do not add capacity just to feel better. Add capacity where it improves delivery in a measurable way.

Step 2: Design the role around output, not personality. Most founders hire too vaguely. I know I did. We too often look for someone "good," "smart," or "hardworking," and then hope the role will define itself over time. That is not how capacity is built. A capacity role should be designed around output. Use this simple template:

- **Primary output:** What does this role produce?

- **Quality standard:** What does "done right" look like?

- **Volume target:** How many per week or month by day 90?

- **Decision rights:** What can they decide without you?

- **Escalation rules:** When do they bring you in?

- **Scoreboard:** What metrics prove success and justify hiring the next capacity role?

If you cannot answer those questions clearly, you are not ready to hire capacity yet. Keep refining the system first.

Step 3: Ramp them to ownership on purpose. Do not throw the role over the wall and hope it works. Capacity hires need a planned ramp. A simple 30/60/90-day framework works well:

- **First 30 days:** Learn the process, shadow the work, and understand the standards

- **Next 30 days:** Begin producing with coaching and review

- **Final 30 days:** Own a defined slice of output with clear reporting and tighter accountability

The goal is not just to get help, even really good help. The goal is to move toward real ownership of the work. That takes repetition. It takes feedback. It takes patience. But if you are serious about building a business that can carry more weight, this is where the work starts to become real.

Step 4: Measure whether the hire is actually creating capacity. Do not leave the success of this role to feel or intuition. Decide in advance how you'll know whether the hire is working. A capacity hire should improve things such as:

- Output volume

- Turnaround time

- Service consistency

- Founder time freed up

- Throughput without a matching rise in founder effort

If none of those are improving, you may not have created capacity yet. You may simply have added payroll.

Step 5: Protect the system you are hiring into. One reason capacity hires fail is that founders hire them into chaos, or something close to it. The new person enters a role with unclear standards, weak processes, inconsistent handoffs, and too many founder-dependent exceptions. Then everyone is disappointed when the hire does not "fix it." That is not the hire's fault.

At this point, you should not be hiring into chaos. You are hiring into a system. That is why the previous Upgrades matter so much; many of these steps support and build on each other. The clearer the service model, the scoreboard, the documented processes, and the decision rights, the faster and more successfully a capacity hire can become productive.

Definition of done: A capacity hire is working when output rises measurably, quality holds, founder dependence shrinks, and the business can grow without founder hours increasing at the same rate.

But adding capacity is not enough by itself. If the founder still keeps the decisions, approvals, and judgment calls, then the business has gained output without gaining much real independence. Capacity is strongest when authority begins to move with it.

And that is where we go next.

★ ★ ★ ★ ★

Build Capacity & Authority
(Year Four: Upgrades 10 Through 12)

Goal of Year Four: Build real carrying power through more deliberate growth, stronger systems, and the first true capacity hire, so the business can handle more demand while gradually freeing up the time of the founder to lead the business.

Review cadence:

☐ Weekly (15 min)

☐ Monthly (30-45 min)

☐ Quarterly (60-90 min)

Date this checklist started: ______________________________

Target "Year Four complete" date: _______________________

UPGRADE NO. 10: BUILD THE GROWTH ENGINE

☐ We have identified one primary growth engine and are working it consistently.

☐ We are measuring key growth inputs and outputs, not just hoping for more revenue.

☐ We can see our pipeline, conversion patterns, and retention more clearly than before.

☐ Growth is becoming more deliberate, visible, and less dependent on founder heroics.

☐ Growth decisions are being made with profitability, capacity, and durability in mind.

☐ The business is less reliant on the founder as the only long-term engine of growth.

Notes:

____

____

____

____

UPGRADE NO. 11: SCALE WITH SYSTEMS

☐ We have clarified what must stay true as the business grows.

☐ We have identified the next major constraint and are addressing it intentionally.

☐ We are strengthening systems before adding more volume.

☐ Our service model, processes, roles, and scoreboard are supporting growth more effectively.

☐ The business can carry more weight with less chaos than before.

☐ Founder involvement is becoming more strategic and less tied to constant hustle.

Notes:

____

____

____

____

UPGRADE NO. 12: MAKE YOUR FIRST CAPACITY HIRE

☐ We have identified the area where added capacity is truly needed.

☐ The role is designed around output, standards, decision rights, and measurable outcomes.

☐ A 30/60/90-day ramp to ownership exists and is being followed.

☐ We know how we will measure whether this hire is creating real capacity.

☐ Output and throughput are improving without founder hours increasing at the same rate.

☐ The hire is being placed into a clear, strong, measured system, not into founder-dependent chaos.

Notes:

____

____

____

____

Year Four "Proof of Progress"

Growth discipline is:

☐ Reactive

☐ Improving

☐ Deliberate

Systems under pressure are:

☐ Fragile

☐ Improving

☐ Stronger

Capacity to carry more demand is:

☐ Tight

☐ Growing

☐ Meaningfully stronger

Founder involvement in growth and delivery is:

☐ Constant

☐ Reduced

☐ More strategic

Business carrying power is:

☐ Limited

☐ Improving

☐ Real and visible

Year Four Reflection (10 minutes)

The most important source of growth we strengthened this year:

____

____

____

The system or bottleneck that improved the most:

____

____

____

The biggest remaining capacity constraint:

____

____

____

The next focus for Year Five:

____

____

____

Printable *Action Guides* for each Upgrade in Year Four are available in the Resources section on my author's website at: https://davidgrausr.com/resources/

* * * * *

Year Five
Build Independence & Options

By Year Five, the business should be stronger and much less dependent on your daily involvement than when you began. This final year is about turning that progress into something more lasting with greater independence, better ownership thinking, and some real options for the future as you consider how best to realize the value you've built.

The three Upgrades in Year Five focus on the founder's final structural shift. First, you transfer authority, not just tasks, so decisions and responsibility no longer keep flowing back to you. Then you begin to think like an owner-investor, with greater attention to what creates durability, value, and long-term return. Finally, you address continuity and succession planning so the business is better prepared for disruption, transition, or eventual transfer.

A note for Path Two readers: Authority, ownership thinking, and continuity planning create options, reduce risk, and make the business more durable even if you remain meaningfully involved. You do not have to go all the way to benefit from going further than you have so far.

UPGRADE NO. 13
Transfer Authority, Not Just Tasks

Why it matters:

- Protects quality as you grow

- Increases business value and transferability

- Delegation without authority creates constraints

- Authority transfer is how you break founder dependence

In the early years, founders delegate tasks to people they hire to help them. That is necessary, but many founders stop there. You know the arguments and the problems at this point, so let's get specific and introduce the elements of this Upgrade.

Authority means having the power to decide, approve, resolve, and move work forward within clear limits. When authority stays centralized at the hub of the wheel, you can hire more people and still remain stuck. When authority begins to transfer, the business becomes less dependent on your presence.

That distinction matters because a business does not become less founder-dependent merely by adding people. It becomes less founder-dependent when the right people can carry real responsibility and move work forward without waiting on the founder every time. That is the point at which added capacity begins to turn into real bench strength. Let's distinguish those terms:

- **Capacity** means we can do more

- **Bench strength** means we can do more, and we can do it well, all without the founder's constant supervision

Bench strength is not only about capable helpers on your team, and it certainly is not only about rainmakers. It is about capable people at multiple levels who can own outcomes so the business continues to grow and get stronger even when, especially when, you step back or are not available.

For context on this journey, think of the progression this way:

- **Upgrade No. 5** adds leverage (hands)

- **Upgrade No. 12** adds capacity (output)

- **Upgrade No. 13** adds independence (capability + authority)

Consider this brief example: Imagine you are a single-owner financial advisory business with a small support team of four helpers. You hire a sharp associate as your first capacity hire. At first, you delegate tasks such as drafting, preparing materials, taking notes, and routine follow-ups. Helpful, but you are still the routing hub.

Upgrade No. 13 is where that changes. Instead of handing off more tasks, you transfer authority tied to outcomes. You assign ownership of a designated set of clients, customers, and functions and define what "done right" looks like in terms of response standards, quality expectations, required deliverables, documentation rules, and escalation boundaries. You coach closely at first, then step back as consistency grows. Mistakes happen, but that is part of the process. The answer is better standards, better training, and clearer limits, not retreating back to the treadmill.

Gradually, the role moves from helper to owner of the process. In this example, the associate no longer just completes tasks; **they own outcomes**. The founder stays involved where it matters most, but the business no longer depends on the founder for every decision and every result, at least as to this group of clients or customers, and functions.

Here is the key distinction-delegation removes work from your hands; authority transfer removes work from your desk. If the work still comes back to you for approval, judgment, or problem-solving, you have delegated tasks, but you have not yet granted authority.

This is also the Upgrade where a business starts looking more credible to a successor, buyer, or investor, because authority is no longer trapped in one person. This is important as, during this Year Five set of Upgrades, we consider internal equity transfers to retain talent, reward initiative, and perpetuate the business. Such durability does not happen by accident or to those lucky enough to build a big business. It has to be designed. Here are five practical ways to begin making that shift.

Step 1: Assign owners, not just helpers. Name three to five critical roles and assign clear ownership. The goal is not to spread work around more loosely. It is to make sure specific outcomes live with specific people.

Step 2: Define "done right." For each role, clarify the outcomes, decision rights, and key metrics. Authority works best when people know what they are responsible for, what standards apply, and how success will be measured.

Step 3: Use an authority ladder. Move decisions from:

- Watch me, to

- Do it with me, to

- Do it and report, to

- Own it!

This is how authority moves gradually and responsibly, without throwing people into work they are not yet prepared to own… or thrusting you into a position where you're not yet prepared for them to own it.

Step 4: Transfer relationships, not just tasks. Clients and customers must learn to trust the business, not only the founder. That means new people need visible ownership, direct contact, and enough authority to handle issues without routing everything back to you.

Step 5: Run the two-week test. If you disappeared for two weeks, what breaks? What stalls? What comes back to you? That test reveals where authority has not really transferred yet.

Definition of done: at this stage, at least one person can run day-to-day operations for two weeks without you, at least one person can lead delivery or quality without you, and founder-only decisions have been reduced to a short list of strategic choices. Most importantly, the business no longer waits for you to make every decision.

As authority begins to move out into the business, the founder's role must change with it. You are no longer just the person doing, approving, and rescuing. You're becoming the owner of an asset that should be more valuable because it is less dependent on you. That requires a new way of thinking, and this is the fun part!

* * * * *

Think Like An Owner-Investor

Why it matters:

- It funds freedom and options

- Wealth is different from income; you can and should build both

- This is the shift from operator thinking to owner-investor thinking

- It makes Upgrade No. 15 (Continuity and Succession Planning) possible

- Your small business may well be the largest, most valuable asset you now own

Most founders think of their business's *value* as the money they take home each month. In a founder-dependent model, that's understandable because the business *is* largely the founder's effort converted into income. But once you build a more founder-independent business, one with systems, a team, growth engines, scale, and repeatable performance, your small business becomes something else entirely.

It becomes an investment that can create wealth in multiple, tax efficient ways. And you own and control it! That requires a different way of thinking – that of an owner AND investor.

To be blunt, this is one of the most powerful financial benefits of becoming an owner-investor in your own well-built small business. I call it the **Owner Wealth Stack** because it provides multiple layers of tax efficient wealth building over the course of your career:

LAYER ONE		WAGES
LAYER TWO	+	PROFIT DISTRIBUTIONS
LAYER THREE	+	EQUITY INCOME (+ INTEREST INCOME)
LAYER FOUR	+	STOCK OR EQUITY APPRECIATION
	=	BUILDING WEALTH

The Owner Wealth Stack is best defined as the cumulative benefits of a growing, profitable, well-structured, founder-independent business, or a more independent business for our many Path Two readers. To be clear, this is a tax-conduit business structure, with equity transferred to next generation buyers/owners over time as part of a Succession Plan (see Upgrade No. 15 for details).

Another way to put it is… *this is what's in it for you!* And the sooner you make the Owner Wealth Stack start working for you, and your family, the better.

To clarify, wages or owner's compensation is earned in exchange for the work you do. Profit distributions are your ROI, or *Return On Investment* of time and capital. Equity income is the money you can receive by selling some of your ownership, or equity, as you get closer to retirement, and if you seller finance it, you can earn interest on the sale as well. And stock or equity appreciation is the increase in value of what you own as your business grows and becomes more profitable and durable.

Depending on your chosen entity structure and geographic location, the layers beyond wages may also come with increasing tax efficiencies (talk with your local tax advisor, or reach out to me – contact link at the end of *A Closing Thought*). The larger point is this. Most treadmill-driven businesses primarily produce Layer One and sometimes Layer Two if you work hard enough. Founder-independent businesses can evolve to produce all four layers over perhaps decades. That can be life changing.

What changes when you start thinking like an owner-investor? You no longer just ask, "How much did I take home this year?". Instead, you start asking, "How much money did I make *and* how much wealth did I build this year?" You will begin to maintain a personal balance sheet, and it helps to explain the reasons you do what you do to those who wish you were home more. This effort is valuable indeed.

Once you understand how the Owner Wealth Stack works for you, the next step is learning what strengthens each layer, and what might quietly erode them. To be clear, for most small business owners, this is your retirement plan if you do it well. Here are some steps to help you monitor and maintain your Owner Wealth Stack:

- Track your value drivers on your scoreboard, such as growth rates, profitability, customer or client retention, concentration risk, bench strength, and capacity.

- Protect margin by controlling overhead and paying yourself (i.e., compensation) intentionally and reasonably.

- Keep building a strong and consistent growth engine and begin shifting it from founder-powered to system-powered.

- Invest where value compounds such as in systems, leadership depth, client experience, and predictable demand.

The point is this: a founder-dependent business can provide a good living as long as you work. A founder-independent business can become a powerful wealth-building asset even as you grow older and begin to throttle back in terms of time in the office. This Upgrade's benefits take effect the moment you start making decisions like an owner-investor, because once you see how wealth through a small business is actually built, you stop needing the treadmill for protection and control… and you start building equity.

And equity is a tool for reshaping the future of your business. That's where we go next as we complete the list of Upgrades.

* * * * *

Address Continuity
And Succession Planning

Why it matters:

- It completes the move off the treadmill

- Protects one of your most valuable assets

- Prevents a crisis from becoming a collapse

- Signals professionalism and long-term planning

- Because surprises happen, and careers can end suddenly

Path Two note: This one is about protection, not ambition.

Technically, a Continuity Plan is a written, legally enforceable set of instructions for what happens if an owner suddenly cannot continue to work due to disability, death, a partnership dispute, or loss of any required licensure.

Practically, think of your Continuity Plan as **Plan B**. Continuity planning is not retirement planning. It's *surprise planning* or, said another way, planning for the inevitable surprises life provides us with as small business owners. It prepares for and answers the questions that otherwise get decided in a panic, such as:

- Who is in charge tomorrow morning?

- Who can sign checks and access accounts?

- Who talks to clients and employees?
- What happens to ownership and control?
- How is the business valued, and how is a buyout funded?

Every small business with two or more owners should have a Buy-Sell Agreement in place. And solo owners need continuity too because while the risk is not a partner conflict, it is about **key-person interruption**. And the more founder-dependent your business is, the harder this is to solve for.

A one-owner business can still create continuity by naming a temporary operator, establishing access and authority rules, and putting a clear path in place for an orderly sale or internal transition if the owner is suddenly unavailable – but, practically, it is hard to do. Think of a Continuity Plan as a seatbelt. You hope you never need it. You put it on anyway.

A formal Succession Plan should be **Plan A**, which also can serve as Plan B at the same time because when you have a younger group of next gen owners, they serve as a natural continuity plan. Succession planning is what you do when you want your business to outlive your daily presence and eventually your career. It is the deliberate process of transitioning leadership and ownership, internally or externally, on a timeline you control.

A Succession Plan ideally transfers equity (think, shares of stock if you're an S-corporation owner) gradually over a decade or more to a younger successor team. As founders, the senior owner or owners retain a controlling interest until they are ready to fully retire and then they sell their remaining interest usually at fair market value to an internal group, usually key employees and even a son or daughter. From a client or customer's perspective, a Succession Plan is a natural progression of the business and its leadership team. It's addition rather than subtraction.

A practical Succession Plan answers these key questions about the future:

1) Who will lead?
2) When does the Plan begin?
3) Who will be the future owner(s)?
4) How will value be transferred and financed?
5) What will the founder do next?

Succession doesn't have to be complicated, but it does have to be intentional. Without a formal plan, most founders don't retire; they slowly burn out, allow clients to leave by attrition, or wait until circumstances force a decision. With a well-crafted Succession Plan, you craft your own options: a phased step-back, an internal sale to people you trust and mentor, a strategic sale (or two, or three) when value is high, or a role change that keeps you engaged without keeping you trapped. I cover all this in much greater detail in a previous book, *Building With the End in Mind.*

If you implement most of these Upgrades, then complete the journey by doing these two final things:

Execute a Plan B – Continuity Plan:

- Identify who takes temporary control if you're suddenly out for 30 to 90 days

- Document access (banking, passwords, key vendors, key accounts, key contacts)

- Document the "what happens next" steps for customers and employees who are depending on your business

- Have your attorney draft the appropriate agreement(s) (i.e., Buy-Sell/Operating/Shareholder provisions), especially if there are multiple owners.

Consider Plan A – Succession Plan:

- Decide your most likely path: internal vs. external

- Name the capabilities the successor (team) must develop

- Set a rough timeline (even if it's 10+ years out)

- Keep building the business so it can transfer systems, bench strength, margin, and reduced founder dependence, rather than a list of clients or assets.

In this context, the founder's treadmill isn't just exhausting. It's risky. A business that depends too heavily on one person can be disrupted, even destroyed, by a single unexpected event. Continuity planning helps protect the business from that risk. Succession planning helps protect your future, realize the value you have built, and extend an ownership opportunity to the next generation of owners and key employees. Together, they complete the transition from a job with overhead to a durable, valuable business that can outlast you and be transferred on your terms.

* * * * *

Build Independence & Options (Year Five: Upgrades 13 Through 15)

Goal of Year Five: Build a business that is more valuable, grow from founder to CEO to owner/investor, and prepare for continuity, succession, and eventual transfer on the founder's terms and timetable.

Review cadence:

☐ Weekly (15 min)

☐ Monthly (30-45 min)

☐ Quarterly (60-90 min)

Date this checklist started: _______________________________

Target "Year Five complete" date: _______________________

UPGRADE NO. 13: TRANSFER AUTHORITY, NOT JUST TASKS

☐ We have named three to five critical roles with clear ownership.

☐ "Done right" is defined for key roles in terms of outcomes, standards, and metrics.

☐ We are using some version of an authority ladder (watch me/do it with me/do it and report/own it).

☐ At least one person has visible ownership of relationships, functions, or outcomes that used to route back through the founder.

☐ The two-week test will go much better than it did three to four years ago.

☐ Founder-only decisions have been reduced to a shorter list of strategic choices.

Notes:

____

____

____

____

UPGRADE NO. 14: THINK LIKE AN OWNER-INVESTOR

☐ I understand the four layers of the Owner Wealth Stack: wages, profit distributions, equity income, and appreciation and how they can and should work for me.

☐ I am seriously thinking more about wealth-building and value creation, not just annual take-home income.

☐ We are tracking key value drivers on the scoreboard (growth, profitability, retention, concentration risk, bench strength, and capacity).

☐ Margin is being protected intentionally through pricing, overhead discipline, and owner compensation decisions.

☐ The business is becoming less key-person dependent and more system-and-team dependent.

☐ I can explain to my family how this business is becoming stronger and more valuable over time.

Notes:

____

____

____

____

UPGRADE NO. 15: ADDRESS CONTINUITY AND SUCCESSION PLANNING

☐ We have identified the essential elements of a Plan B continuity plan.

☐ Key access, control, and "what happens next" information is documented and organized.

☐ If there are multiple owners, the appropriate legal agreement(s) are in place or underway.

☐ We have identified our most likely Plan A succession path.

☐ We have named the capabilities a future successor or successor team must develop.

☐ We have at least a rough timeline for continuity and succession planning, even if the transition is many years away.

Notes:

____

____

____

____

Year Five "Proof of Independence"

Authority in the business is:

☐ Founder-centered

☐ Improving

☐ Meaningfully shared

Owner thinking is:

☐ Income-focused

☐ Expanding

☐ Wealth-focused

Continuity readiness is:

- ☐ Weak

- ☐ Improving

- ☐ Credible

Succession readiness is:

- ☐ Distant

- ☐ Emerging

- ☐ Taking shape

Founder dependence overall is:

- ☐ High

- ☐ Reduced

- ☐ Meaningfully reduced

- ☐ Eliminated

Year Five Reflection (10 minutes)

The most important authority shift we made this year:

____

____

____

The biggest value driver we understand better now:

____

____

____

The most important continuity or succession gap still remaining:

____

____

____

What I want this business to make possible next:

____

____

____

Printable *Action Guides* for each Upgrade in Year Five are available in the Resources section on my author's website at: https://davidgrausr.com/resources/

* * * * *

LOOKING BACK

One of the benefits I hope to share with you is a sense of perspective. As I move through the second half of my sixties, and after a 30+ year career as a small business owner, I've spent time looking up the mountain, and now back down those slopes. I worked on my craft every day for decades and now I have the time to think and write about my experiences.

As you know, I took Path Three. I built a fully founder-independent business using most of the fifteen Upgrades in this field guide. I grew my business significantly, made a great deal of money, completed a full succession plan, and sold out. On paper, it worked beautifully. In very real ways, it worked in life too. I used some of the proceeds to buy my wife the horse farm and land she had always dreamed of. She drinks coffee every morning with her two horses, and that gives me real joy. I am proud of that.

But would I do it the same way again? No. I don't think I would.

If I had it to do over, I think I would choose Path Two, and pull from most of the Upgrades, but over about ten years. I'd find a way to keep my sons in the business if they wanted to stay. I'd take even better care of my team.

I've been leaving hints about that choice throughout this book, especially for the Path Two readers. At times, those readers may have felt like they were standing just outside the spotlight while I kept building toward the full founder-independent model. But the truth is, some of those breadcrumbs were for me too. I was trying to better understand what I might have done differently, and what success has actually cost me.

I still remember the day I bought out my last partner. He handed me the signed documents, smiled, and said, "Your job is to one day make yourself irrelevant. That will be the smartest thing you ever do." We both laughed, nervously, but I never forgot the advice. In many ways, that sentiment shaped everything that followed. It was part of what pushed me to bring in outside help and build a business with real structure, real independence, and real value.

And I did exactly that. But there was a cost.

I used to walk into the office every day with a smile on my face. I loved most of the people I worked with and thought of many of them as good friends. The business was my life. But over time, I traded some of that closeness for a bigger, stronger, more valuable business. When I sold the last of my equity, I left my old team behind, and we no longer talk much. Along the way, both of my sons, who worked a combined eighteen years in the business, left angrily. They did not like the direction I was taking our operations. Our relationships have never been the same.

That's hard to admit, but it's true.

After thirty years, I also miss something else: I miss being the most important person in the room. I miss walking into the office and feeling the weight of my role before I ever said a word. I miss the respect, the authority, the history, and yes, even the power. I miss knowing that, in a hard conversation or during a difficult week, my presence alone changed the outlook of the room. I really liked being the founding owner. It felt good to matter that much.

That may not be noble, but it is honest, and I need to offer that sense of perspective.

So if you are reading this book and finding yourself drawn more to Path Two than Path Three, do not assume that you're aiming too low. You may simply be choosing more carefully and more purposefully than I did. Path Three can absolutely work. I know because I lived it. But it's not free, and the price is not always – or just financial. Sometimes the price is relational. Sometimes it's personal. Sometimes it is bound up in identity, control, and the quiet human pleasure of being deeply needed.

Having walked the full Path Three journey, I think I would choose differently next time. Not because I regret building something valuable, but because I now better understand what I was giving up in exchange. I would still want a strong, profitable, durable business. But I think I would keep more of what I once had – not more money, but more closeness, more control, more daily meaning, and more of the life inside the business that made the journey feel worthwhile in the first place.

No one should ever feel irrelevant, and that's part of my truth. You deserve to hear it.

* * * * *

LEARNING TO BE AN OWNER (AND CEO)

The third and final part of this field guide is about the shift that happens after you have installed the necessary structure and Upgrades. It is about learning to live and lead as an owner, not a crisis manager.

We will also confront something almost no one talks about: relapse. This is the moment stress, urgency, or fear tempts you back onto the treadmill and convinces you that it would be faster, safer, or easier if you just did it yourself. We will name that impulse, normalize it, and build a simple way to recover quickly without surrendering the structure you worked so hard to build.

One important reminder before we begin: you don't need to become fully founder-independent to benefit from what you have built to date, and you do not need to complete every Upgrade in exactly five years. Many readers will land somewhere in the middle, on Path Two, and that is a worthy destination. Some Upgrades may simply be more than your business needs. Focus on implementing what works for you, and keep strengthening the improvements you have already made.

If the first section of this field guide helped you see the treadmill for what it is, and the second helped you build your way off it – or at least slow it down and loosen its grip – this final section is about learning how to stay off it, or mostly stay off it, and make good use of what you have earned, and learned.

CHAPTER SIX

Stepping Off The Treadmill

This chapter is not a victory lap. Stepping off the founder's treadmill rarely feels like instant freedom. More often, it feels like discomfort, uncertainty, and the strange loss of a role you have lived for years.

That may sound odd, especially after all the work it takes to build a stronger, less founder-dependent business. But it is true. When your business begins to rely less on your constant effort, you do not just change the structure. You change your relationship to the business itself.

For years, your control has likely come through personal effort. You knew what was happening because you touched it, approved it, fixed it, or carried it yourself. If sacrifice had a storefront, it would be a small business built by hands that never seem to rest. But as the Upgrades take hold, that kind of control will begin to give way to something different: **control through structure.**

At first, that can feel slower, less satisfying, and even a little threatening. You may wonder whether quality is slipping, whether anyone cares as much as you do, or whether the old way was better after all. Those feelings are normal. They are also often misleading. Being needed can feel gratifying. Being the one with all the answers can feel powerful. But neither is the foundation of a durable, valuable business.

Structure feels slower at first because it requires patience, repetition, and trust. But over time, it creates what personal effort alone rarely can: calm, consistency, and the ability to lead without constantly rescuing.

Accept that **relapse is normal**. Most founders don't step off the treadmill just once. They step off, then back on, then off again. That is not failure. It is part of unwinding that part of a business that has been organized around you for years. Relapse is normal, especially when stress rises and the old way still feels faster, or at least more certain and comfortable. Relapse usually happens for one of three reasons:

1) **Stress hits.** A cash squeeze, a major client issue, a key employee leaves, or something urgent demands immediate action.

2) **Standards slip.** Someone does not do it "your way," an important client complains loudly, and you decide it is better, and quicker, just to take it back.

3) **Control feels safer than coaching.** Teaching takes time and it requires a diligent student. Doing it yourself feels efficient, at least in the moment.

The danger is not stepping back on briefly. The danger is staying there because it feels familiar, effective, or safe. So here is the rule: **when relapse happens, treat it as a signal, not a surrender.**

Ask yourself, "What broke?!" Was it people, process, decision rights, training, or the scoreboard? Or something else? Whatever it was, fix that part. Hand the work back. Then try again.

If you keep the work, you keep the treadmill and the limitations that come with it. A less founder-dependent business is not built by never relapsing. It is built by relapsing less, recovering faster, and strengthening the structure each time. It is hard to be great when doing something for the first time.

Outside perspective helps here. This is also the point at which outside perspective becomes especially valuable. Founders are often too close to the work to see the pattern clearly when they feel the need to slip back into rescue mode. This is where a good coach, advisor, peer group, or seasoned operator can help. Not because you are broken or undisciplined, but because you are inside the system you are trying to redesign. That is hard to do.

An experienced, calm, and dispassionate voice can help you spot recurring patterns, clarify the next right step, and hold you accountable to building structure instead of sliding back into founder heroics. The point is, don't be afraid to ask for some help. Chances are it will speed up the process and result in fewer setbacks, or of shorter duration.

Founder-led is not the same as founder-trapped. Let me reiterate something important as we begin the process of looking back on what has been learned. The point of this field guide is not to convince every reader to disappear from their business or work less hard. It is to help you stop being required for everything. That is a very different goal:

- **Founder-led** means "I am deeply involved because I want to be."

- **Founder-trapped** means "I am deeply involved because I have to be."

That distinction matters.

You do not have to "escape" the treadmill completely to win and build something meaningful. Even if you plan to remain meaningfully involved, you can still step away from the parts of the business that create the most stress, the least leverage, and the greatest fragility.

A handful of the Upgrades may be enough to buy back time, reduce pressure, improve margins, build reserves, and create real options without turning your business into a total reinvention project.

If you genuinely like being at the center of the business, that's fine. There is no shame in building a "small and strong" company that supports your life. To this end, even a founder-led business should still have:

- An entity and tax structure that makes sense

- Cash-flow discipline and reserves

- Written processes for critical routines

- A service model that reduces exceptions

- Basic continuity and succession planning

This isn't empire-building; it's responsible ownership. Because here's the truth: the risks do not disappear just because you like your current model. Illness, burnout, family needs, and market changes happen to everyone, and usually without permission. The best gift you can give yourself, your team, and your future is a business that can absorb stress without breaking.

What real ownership starts to feel like. As your business grows stronger, your role will change. You will still lead. You still will make key decisions. You may still stay deeply involved in the work that matters most to you.

The goal is not to vanish. The goal is to stop being required for everything. That's what real ownership feels like. The next, natural question is what that looks like in practice, especially when founders begin thinking about working remotely, spending more time away, or moving toward so-called absentee ownership. What are your real choices as you begin to get some important time back?

That's where we go next.

* * * * *

CHAPTER SEVEN

Remote vs. Absentee Ownership

Absentee ownership is rarely the result of moving from founder-dependent to founder-independent, or even something in between. Founder-independent means the business no longer funnels every decision through you. It does not mean you get to disappear from the business.

Before we accept or reject the idea, let's clearly define the terms. "Absentee ownership" gets used loosely and is widely applied, but it usually means one of two very different things:

1) **Remote ownership (still involved).** You're not in the office every day, but you're still actively engaged. You may work remotely some days, travel more, or visit periodically, while still leading through systems, metrics, and people. This is realistic for many businesses once the bulk of the Upgrades are substantially in place.

2) **True absentee ownership (not involved in daily operations).** In this instance, you are largely removed from day-to-day management. You are an investor-owner, more than an operator-owner. That requires someone else to lead daily activities, such as an on-site CEO or general manager with real authority and business experience. Without that leader, absentee ownership of a small business can quickly become neglect.

Those are two very different approaches.

What is realistic for most small businesses? Modern tools make remote work possible, and the pandemic not only proved that but spurred the creation of new tools and enhanced existing ones. But here's the reality: for most founders, their ownership interest represents their single largest, most valuable asset, and often their primary income stream as well. The smaller the business, the more important it is that leadership is present and engaged, on-site, more days than not.

Founder-independence may allow you to work remotely on Fridays, travel more freely and frequently during vacation season, or be out of the office for a week or two at a time, or more, without panic. That's a win. That is absolutely one of the purposes of the preceding Upgrades. But in my experience, for most businesses under 25 people, total absence is rarely sustainable without a true on-site leader.

As businesses grow (think 50 people or more), bench strength deepens, systems mature, leadership layers form, and things begin to change. At some point, more time away becomes realistic without profitability, growth, or quality suffering. But the principle stays the same: **Somebody must lead daily.** If it isn't you, it must be someone else with the authority to act and the experience to lead. In my own business, once it got to this size, we began to fill out our C-suite, adding a Chief Financial Officer, a Chief Operating Officer, and so on. This group was also allowed to buy into equity ownership and did a wonderful job of keeping things running when the senior owners were not around. It really makes a difference when your talent, leaders, and key employees are fully invested. Oftentimes there is just no better way to help next gen talent learn to *think like an owner* than to write a check every month.

Why absentee ownership often fails in smaller firms: The fifteen Upgrades as part of the Five-Year Plan are not check-the-box activities. They require maintenance, because over time, standards drift, key people leave, markets change, new competitors emerge, and systems need refinement. A business left unattended doesn't stay stable. It slowly degrades, often quietly, until something significant breaks.

And there's another issue to consider. In a small firm, hiring a CEO-level leader can be expensive. It costs money, yes, but it can also cost clarity and culture. If your margins don't support it, absentee ownership can reduce profitability more than it increases freedom. That's why most small business owners don't become absentee. Instead, they become something much better: **founder-independent and founder-led.**

When true absentee ownership can work: There are models I've worked with in which near-absentee ownership can work well, especially when a single, well-structured business operates through multiple locations as might be the case when there are multiple business acquisitions occurring. In these cases, the owner builds a repeatable playbook and installs an on-site leader at each location. The owner's job becomes that of recruiting leaders, reviewing metrics, protecting standards, and intervening only when needed. It can work very well, but only when leadership depth and accountability systems are strong across the board.

Final thoughts: Founder-independence buys you choice. Absenteeism is a different business model.

* * * * *

CHAPTER EIGHT

Leadership (In A Nutshell)

Many founders spend the first years of their business reacting to whatever the day demands. The phone rings. A dozen emails come in. A client or customer needs immediate help. An employee has a quick question, or two. Ultimately, when a problem arises, the founder solves it.

That is survival, not leadership, even as heroic as the efforts might be.

Once you implement some or all of the fifteen Upgrades, something important begins to happen. You no longer have only a job to perform. You have a business to run, complete with systems, profits, growth, value, and a stronger team to work with. And somewhere along the way, whether you're ready or not, you become the leader. That shift matters.

You may have noticed that none of the fifteen Upgrades are called "Learn How to Lead." That's because leadership is harder to reduce to a worksheet or a checklist. The Upgrades are tools. They help you build structure, capacity, accountability, and independence. But once those tools are in place, **the founder has to evolve.** The goal is not merely to work less hard. It's to use the time and capacity you have gained to lead wisely, teach effectively, and think ahead on behalf of everyone who is depending on you. If ownership is what you hold, leadership is what you carry for everyone else.

Installing the Upgrades will not result in a system on autopilot or cruise control. Systems drift. Standards soften. People leave. New employees misunderstand what matters. Markets change. Competitors emerge. Problems reappear in new forms. The structure you built must now be led, reinforced, and improved. That is the founder's new work. You are no longer carrying the entire business on your back every day. Instead, you are setting the direction, protecting standards, developing people, and making sure the system keeps working when life gets noisy again.

I can tell you from experience that this step is not automatic. It probably will not feel normal right away. Most of us were not born knowing how to lead. We learn by doing, by making decisions, by getting some of them wrong, and by growing into the responsibility over time. And yes, there is a certain irony here. You build a stronger, less founder-dependent business so that you can stop carrying everything yourself, only to discover that you now have a different and, arguably, a more demanding responsibility!

Leadership requires courage almost every day. You will be required to make decisions without perfect information. You will have to choose a direction when most others are unsure, skeptical, or afraid. Sometimes you will need to act long before the outcome is clear. That is part of the job. Make the call.

I found that the work I enjoyed doing was not the strategic leadership role of a CEO. I enjoyed working more closely, if not directly, with our clients, teaching, consulting, and writing. So, I brought in an outside CEO to perform that role and I took on the title of "President and Founder," which suited me just fine. In the years that followed, we advanced others into the positions of Chief Operating Officer and Chief Financial Officer Because there isn't much room for overlapping roles in a small, fast growing business (not to say that one person can't do several jobs), it often helps to put the specific duties of each leader into writing in your Operating Agreement or Partnership Agreement. This process can also help you understand better why problems creep up that aren't being addressed regularly or properly.

As you gradually embrace the role of CEO, if not the title (and, at least early on, many of the other officer roles as well!), your work changes in an important way. You're new role will be to make sure the business knows where it is going, how it is supposed to operate, and is prepared for what happens next. At this stage, five leadership duties matter most:

1) **You prepare for the future.** This includes risk, continuity, succession, leadership depth, and long-term value. As CEO, your job is trying to make sure the business can survive setbacks, handle growth, and function with increasing strength over time. That means building systems, reducing key-person dependence, developing successors, and making the business more durable than it was a year ago. Constant improvement and refinement of systems and processes is required.

2) **You reinforce the standards.** Culture is no longer just the founder's personality. It becomes a lived pattern of what gets rewarded, tolerated, corrected, and repeated. The CEO is responsible for reinforcing what kind of business you're running, how decisions get made, what "done right" means, how people treat each other, and what is not acceptable even if it produces short-term results.

3) **You coach instead of rescue.** On the treadmill, founders solve problems personally because that is the fastest way to get through the day. In a more durable business, not every issue should end with your answer. Many should end with someone else growing stronger. Leadership means assembling a good team and helping them think efficiently, decide properly, and own more without turning every hard moment into a rescue operation.

4) **You review patterns, not just incidents.** A founder-dependent business trains the owner to react to events one at a time. Leadership means stepping back far enough to see the patterns underneath the events. You watch the numbers, the service issues, the repeated bottlenecks, the missed handoffs, the strain on people, and the early signs of drift. You ask questions while the answers are still useful.

5) **You allocate resources.** Time, money, talent, and attention are always limited. The CEO decides where those resources go. Should the business hire now or wait? Invest in sales capacity or operational systems? Push growth or protect margin? Open a second location, add a service line, or tighten the current model first? In a smaller company, resource decisions are often felt immediately. A wrong hire, wrong investment, or wrong priority can affect the whole company. The CEO has to allocate scarce resources with discipline.

That is leadership in a more founder-independent business. Less reacting, more directing. Less rescuing, more reinforcing. Less being the system, more leading the system. As you learn how to handle your new leadership role, you might find it beneficial to form or to join a study group of five or six other CEO's so that you can listen and learn, even commiserate.

The founder's new cadence. If you are wondering what all this looks like in practice, it is usually much less dramatic than in the early years of being a founding owner. Leadership at this stage is not about constant motion. It is about rhythm.

Each week, ask yourself:

- Are we clear on the top priorities right now?

- Are the right people owning the right work?

- Where is the system working, and where is it drifting?

- Who needs coaching instead of rescue?

- What decisions still truly require me?

- What can I reinforce this week that will reduce founder-dependence over time?

Each month, step back and review:

- Key numbers

- Team performance

- Service consistency

- Recurring bottlenecks

- Priorities for the month ahead

- Any problem that keeps repeating itself, even in slightly different forms

This is not glamorous work, but it is essential work. Leadership is not another treadmill. It is the discipline of staying engaged without becoming the bottleneck again. Use your monthly scoreboard to monitor and measure your progress as a business, and your role as the leader of that business. Write down your goals, track your progress or lack thereof, and hold yourself accountable.

Leadership is not ownership. Ownership does not automatically make someone a *good* leader. Plenty of owners are still reacting, rescuing, controlling, and improvising long after the business has grown past the point where that model makes sense. Owning the equity is one thing. Leading the enterprise is another. You have to work to master this craft just like anything else you do. You'll likely spend the rest of your career improving.

In my own founder-dependent businesses, people would sometimes ask, "What does David Sr. want?" At first, I took some pride in hearing that. Years later, I would stop and correct the speaker – in a durable organization, the better question is, "What does the business require?" That is not a small shift. It is one of the biggest shifts the support team of a founder-independent business will ever make. Pleasing the owner is no longer the goal; your team members must learn to look past you to the business that employs them.

Leadership is how the business keeps moving forward *after* the Upgrades are in place. The Upgrades help you build a stronger business. Leadership is what keeps that business aligned, improving, and responsive as conditions change. Use the monthly scoreboard to measure progress, set clear goals, and lead your team in understanding what's working, what's not, and what needs to happen next. You don't have to have all the answers, but you do have to create the conditions in which good answers can emerge. Blame rarely improves the scoreboard. Clarity, accountability, and steady leadership often do.

To this end, many of the Upgrades required or recommended that you get specific and be clear about what you want, what you expect, and where you want to take the business. **Do not be hard to follow.** Encouragement is part of the job, but the most important part is to make the way forward clear. In a strong business, people should not have to guess about what matters or wonder what you really want. That is one of the quiet marks of good leadership.

And that leads to one final, deeply personal question: as you succeed in building a stronger, more profitable, more independent business, how do you want *your story* to end?

* * * * *

CHAPTER NINE

How Does Your Story End?

Will you sell your small business to the highest bidder, or maybe to the best match? Will you keep it and enjoy the income and control for as long as you can? Will you transition it gradually to a son or daughter, or to a small group of key employees? Or do nothing at all and simply work until the day you don't?

There is no wrong answer. It is your business after all. But there are consequences to not deciding.

One of the most important questions I ask founders, often in their forties or fifties, is this: **How do you see your story ending?** Not next year. Not when growth slows, but when you're sixty or seventy, or simply feel you've achieved enough. That final choice isn't decades away – it's shaped in this moment, by what you do – or don't do, today.

Most entrepreneurs start their business careers with a lot of energy, urgency, even a dream to fulfill. Very few start with the end in mind. But every journey ends somewhere. The question is whether you arrive there by design… or by default. If the ending of your story has a shape, it is being built by the choices you make while you still think you have plenty of time. It's my hope that this humble field guide helps you adjust your trajectory just enough that in ten to twenty years, you'll find yourself in a stronger position – ready to seize opportunities and shape the future you want.

And remember: your story and your business's story are not the same, even though they may feel intertwined today. **Your career will come to an end – but your business doesn't have to.** That matters to your employees, and often your customers or clients. That distinction changes everything if you consider and plan for it early enough.

Many founders who earn a good living assume they will just work as long as possible. There's nothing wrong with loving what you do, enjoying the control, or valuing the income. But loving the work and depending on it are two different positions. A durable, well-structured business gives you some important options to take advantage of, and include the ability to:

- Slow down gradually

- Step back without stepping away

- Continue earning wages and profits

- Grow your equity and eventually turn it into a successful exit

- Reduce your hours without reducing your relevance

These positive and rewarding endings, or transitions, do not happen accidentally. Hope is not a plan. These options are the result of years, sometimes decades, of building and planning, often long before you feel you need them. And they rarely emerge within a purely founder-dependent model – at least not beyond one of the options listed above.

Over time, I've learned something humbling: goals that depend only on me are smaller than goals that depend on others through shared leadership, specialized skill sets, and good systems. That is why I've always tried to surround myself with people who are better than me, at least in their areas of specialty. In the end, we made each other better, and together we grew beyond what I could have ever accomplished alone.

Sometimes, as founders, we set goals that are too small because it feels good and necessary to reach them. "I'll have a good job." "I'll make a solid living." "I'll retire comfortably." All worthwhile goals. But there is another question worth considering, not for ego, but for durability and service beyond self: **why not build something that still serves people long after you step away?** Your employees, clients, community, and other stakeholders are affected by how your story ends – and they care. They can only hope that you do.

So let's get that legal pad back out.

Take the time you need to write down how you would like your story to end. Be specific and don't focus solely on financial goals, though those certainly are key factors. Here are some prompts to get you started:

- How many hours a week are you working at age 65?

- Who is running the company day to day at that point?

- How (well) are you compensated?

- How much equity will you continue to own?

- Do you have a goal in mind for business value at that time?

- What will you be doing? What will be your title?

- Where will you be working from? (corner office, remotely, other side of the world)

- What does a Monday morning in February look like to you?

Once you've finished writing, date it and put it aside. Revisit it months, even years later, perhaps on a quiet Sunday afternoon when the noise of the week has faded. Let the calm, long view guide you, not the highs of a great month or the stress of a bad one. And share those goals with the person who will live that ending with you or that has a personal stake in your future. And then listen carefully to their thoughts. Your story's ending affects a lot of other people. Let that be a driving force.

Finally, a common response I hear from successful owners is that they want to monetize the value of what they built upon retirement. Selling is one important option. I thought about it many times myself. Surprisingly, however, it is not the top priority for most founder-independent small businesses. Over 30 years of asking entrepreneurs, "How does your story end?", **eight out of ten** told me they wanted to build something that outlived them, rewarded key staff with an ownership opportunity, took care of their clients, and allowed them to retire on their own terms – if that were possible.

A goal such as this usually occurs when equity is sold over time, often to a family member or a small group of key employees. That is the definition of a Succession Plan. For more on this topic, see my best-selling book, *Building With the End in Mind*, or visit www.davidgrausr.com for additional resources.

A final point: a succession plan doesn't begin five years before retirement. It begins the day you decide your business should be able to move on without you – the day you discover your team is willing to invest their time, their careers, and perhaps even their own capital in the business you've built together. That's a good problem to have.

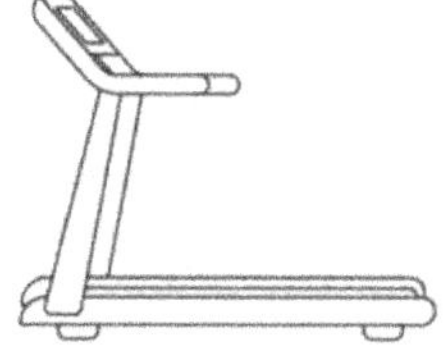

A CLOSING THOUGHT

If you've made it this far, you've already accomplished something very important: you paused long enough to think differently about your business, your role in it, and what you may want it to become. That alone puts you further ahead than you may realize.

The founder's treadmill usually does not end all at once. Most of us don't leap off of it! It ends through a series of small, deliberate choices over the course of at least several years that gradually move the weight of the business off of you and into a structure built to carry it. That takes dedication. It takes effort. And it takes a willingness to do some work now in order to create a better future later.

My hope is that this book has given you both language and direction – language for the trap so many founders struggle to describe or explain, and direction for building something stronger, more durable, and less dependent on you over time.

You don't have to do it all at once. You just have to begin. And if you ever want a thoughtful conversation about your next steps, you're welcome to reach out to me-contact information below.

Thank you for reading, and for caring enough about your business, your people, and your future, to do what it takes to make this work.

David Sr.

PostScript: If you enjoyed this field guide, please consider leaving an honest review on your favorite store or book distribution center. I would appreciate it very much.

If you'd like help thinking through next steps, you can schedule a complimentary and confidential call at **davidgrausr.com/consulting** or by scanning the QR code below:

ABOUT THE AUTHOR

David Grau Sr., JD is a small business "mechanic" with a law degree. He helps founders turn owner-dependent jobs into durable businesses by applying modern systems, financial discipline, leadership depth, and transferable value.

David Sr. began as a force of one, hanging out his own shingle as a securities attorney. Like many founders, he initially enjoyed the freedom of working for himself until he realized he had built a very demanding job, not a business.

He later founded and led a national professional services firm, expanding from two employees to more than sixty owners and staff, supported by fully developed operations including marketing and sales functions. The firm specialized in business valuation (completing over 15,000 valuations during his tenure), continuity and succession planning, and transaction support for financial professionals. David Sr. eventually executed his own succession plan, selling his equity incrementally to an internal successor team, allowing the business to thrive and move on without him – which is exactly how it's supposed to work!

Today, David Sr. writes and consults on building businesses that last and make a difference – and how founders can step off their own treadmill by installing the right structures: sound entity design, disciplined cash-flow systems, strong controls, scalable service models, growth engines, and more. He's the author of multiple books on business-building and perpetuation strategies, including the best-selling series *Building With the End in Mind* and *Acquiring Your Future...* for both generations of the process. He previously wrote a monthly column for *Financial Planning Magazine* for six years, covering succession, business perpetuation, equity management, and valuation.

When he isn't writing and consulting, David Sr. enjoys life as an owner-operator of an equestrian property in the horse capital of America, where his wife serves as the CEO and he provides critical support in the accounting department (or whatever else needs to be done).

Learn more at: **www.davidgrausr.com**

APPENDIX
ADDITIONAL TOOLS

The following are available as print-ready, free downloads at: https://davidgrausr.com/resources/. Each *Action Guide* is a detailed 7 to 10-page worksheet to help you put *pen to paper*, so to speak, and make this process real.

- DURABILITY SELF CHECK WORKSHEET
- ACTION GUIDE FOR UPGRADE NO. 1
- ACTION GUIDE FOR UPGRADE NO. 2
- ACTION GUIDE FOR UPGRADE NO. 3
- ACTION GUIDE FOR UPGRADE NO. 4
- ACTION GUIDE FOR UPGRADE NO. 5
- ACTION GUIDE FOR UPGRADE NO. 6
- ACTION GUIDE FOR UPGRADE NO. 7
- ACTION GUIDE FOR UPGRADE NO. 8
- ACTION GUIDE FOR UPGRADE NO. 9
- ACTION GUIDE FOR UPGRADE NO. 10
- ACTION GUIDE FOR UPGRADE NO. 11
- ACTION GUIDE FOR UPGRADE NO. 12
- ACTION GUIDE FOR UPGRADE NO. 13
- ACTION GUIDE FOR UPGRADE NO. 14
- ACTION GUIDE FOR UPGRADE NO. 15